PSYCHIATRIC TISSUES

JEFF SCHNEIDER

PSYCHIATRIC TISSUES

Published by Pig Roast Publishing, LLC.
www.pigroastpublishing.com

"Noise Terrorists" courtesy of Tim Shannon
Interview courtesy of Sean Carnage
Sunshine for Shady People review courtesy of Kevin McCaighy

Front cover photo: Kristen "Krissy" Arnold (2010)
Back cover photo: Jen Strickland

ISBN: 978-0999407318

PIG ROAST PUBLISHING LLC.

PSYCHIATRIC TISSUES

A memoir by

Jeff Schneider

This book is to be read in a Providence accent.

CONTENTS

Prologue

Arab On Radar
Perfect Sound Forever

"Noise Terrorists"
by Tim Shannon
December 2007

Is there a part deep down inside of you that craves dissonant music? Did you hear the No New York compilation and, not being fully satisfied, demand more? Lament the No Wave scene for being cut down in its prime? Want Sonic Youth to release something like the dark primalness of the Kill Yr Idols EP again? Want music that is worth the risk of potential hearing loss? Feel alienated by what's passing for music nowadays? Is radio leaving you bored with its "safeness"? Do you wonder whatever happened to that underlying, dangerous, threatening, offensive appeal that rock could have, which would scare your parents away? Where's the music to challenge your ear, which you won't find on MTV?

If any of this is hitting a note, you might be a noise fan, and I have good news. Your favorite music hasn't become something extinct like dinosaurs or the optimism of the sixties. Let me be the first to open you eyes to one of the best bands to happen to noise rock in years: Arab on Radar.

No Wave's origins began in New York as a gob in the eye of some of the punk bands who toned down and compromised their sound to look for success, becoming reborn as new wave bands. No Wave pushed the anything-goes ethics of punk further than punks themselves--who sometimes were as conventional as the thing they were rebelling against. Unfortunately, it eventually collapsed as there wasn't enough to sustain its existence. At the end of the 1990's, commercial radio was dominated by the sickening, plastic teen pop phenomenon. Underground music reacted distinctly to all that crap again.

After decades of Sonic Youth and the Swans keeping the flame alive, No Wave started finding favor again, inspiring and influencing new bands to pick up instruments. Besides Arab on Radar, bands like Black Dice, Lightning Bolt, The Locust, Lake of Dracula, Wolf Eyes, and Pink Brown were formed, seemingly coming out of nowhere. These bands were much noisier and more dissonant than the hardest of the hardcore bands of the 1980s, making Black Flag look like the Knack. The bands shared a penchant for experimental music, strange lyrics, and playing anywhere, including warehouses or abandoned buildings. Truly the best part about this No Wave resurgence was that this time it was much better received by people. Positive encouragement of the music allowed them to grow and be able to tour--something that the original No Wave bands couldn't have dreamed of. There's also the benefit of no crossover appeal to ruin the integrity of the musicians.

As Arab On Radar aren't your typical band, neither are their beginnings. Not only did the band members not know each other, but no one had even played in a band before, making their eventual output all the more impressive. It all began in 1994, when four of the members were applying for jobs at a submarine manufacturing company in Connecticut. None of them got the job, but the grueling hiring tests left them all as friends. They went out to a bar and at the end of the night decided to start a band. A woman at the bar named Andrea Fisset enthused about playing bass and was drafted as the fifth member of their band. The band consisted of Eric Paul (vocals), Jeff Schneider (guitar), Stephen Mattos (guitar), Andrea Fisset (bassist) and Craig Kureck (drums). They never went by these names while in the band, opting instead for Mr. Post Traumatic Stress Disorder (aka Paul), Mr.Pottymouth (also aka Paul), Mr.Clinical Depression (aka Schneider), Mr.Type A (aka Mattos), and Mr. Obsessive Compulsive Disorder (aka Kureck, while Fisset didn't have a nickname). They did this to make sure the music was given greater importance and the band members were seen as secondary.

Musically, the band was inspired by the Providence's Six Finger Satellite, Butthole Surfers, US Maple, PiL's Metal Box and the eccentric genius of Captain Beefheart. Early singles like "Inventor," "Aisle 5," and "Kangaroo" are abrasive, owing a serious debt to No Wave while somehow being catchy at the same time. The bass is often at the center to provide some sort of melody while everything else twists, bends and fights around it.

In 1997, they released their first album Queen Hygiene II, on the Providence label Heparin Records, and it showed that they already had a unique form all their own. Paul's trademark lyrics were already in place ("Her underwear has April showers and I'm pissing on her mayflowers"), justifying his pseudonym of Mr. Pottymouth. The guitars on this record sound equally if not more disturbing than the lyrics. A squealing, high-pitched riff incites you to move around and have fun in "Attack on Tijuana" before the guitars spiral off into something more rigid. There's a genius matchup of heavy buzzing bass, a stuttering drumbeat, and a skeletal, jabbing guitar on "St. Patrick's Gay Parade," one of the best songs on the record. "Rubber Robot" is in a constant state of building up while one guitar sounds like a cat being strangled and the other shakes with tenseful fury. This debut is good and isn't that far removed from the singles released around then.

Their second album, 1998's Rough Day at The Orifice (Boston's OpPoPop), finds them moving away from that direction and doing something different. The bass no longer has a flowing riff, instead changing to a tougher, more dirge-like sound. The songs take a heavier, darker tone, and are at times almost drone-like. The sound is more experimental, breaking down song structure and sounding more disjointed then ever. Some good tracks like "Menstruating Thrills," "His Maintenance," and "Biggest Little Prick in The Union," give the album reason for repeated plays. Ultimately though, this album suffers from not having as many good ideas on it as Queen Hygiene II.

Following Rough Day, Andrea Fisset left the band, but that didn't slow them down. Arab on Radar went touring across Europe with the Flying Luttenbachers and had appreciative crowds. On that European tour, they recorded a new album which Weasel Walter (Flying Luttenbachers) would later produce. Coming back to America, their association with Weasel Walter led them to sign with Skin Graft. This was a great advantage for the band. "We got to go to Europe, make a beautiful record, and were saved from an awful record deal that we made (by mistake) with a shitty label in Providence, RI. Skin Graft saved our lives and our record. We helped them stay active as a label... so it all worked out perfect," said Jeff Schneider.

Their third album, Soak The Saddle, was released in 2000, and they sound reinvigorated and energetic on it. Walter's production adds a huge improvement, giving the songs a livelier and punky sound. The tracks on the album may not have names, but they are far from forgettable. On track #1, the drums came right out at you with a punch and the guitars seem like they will tear through the song at any moment. The guitars gasp for air, sounding strung out and unpredictable like a junkie on track #5. The album title coming from track #4 assures us that although the band is progressing they haven't lost their love for shocking lyrics ("Judy Garland doesn't use tampons") with a messy background of sound. Track #9 has a jittery, wild guitar that flies all over the place like a loose, high-powered firehose. Soak the Saddle shows the band moving away from their more straight-ahead material and taking the music to a place without barriers.

Their next album, Yahweh or The Highway (2001), would be their crowning achievement. It's their most realized, creative work and has everyone playing at peak performance. Yahweh throws out the rules to invent this gloriously fucked up music. Looking at the track titles can only give you a hint of the wildness of the music inside. "My Mind is a Muffler" pushes off with a brutish bass riff around screeching abstract guitar, which give way to an industrial factory kind of noise at the end. Dementedly sung lyrics ("Sometimes I just gotta jerk off, my nuts are a pressure cooker") mark a new height of dirtiness for Eric Paul. "Cocaine Mummy" sounds like the audio equivalent of trying to run away with a broken leg while someone blasts a shotgun at you. "God is Dad" starts with a bang, shooting out the gate with guitars swarming like angry bees, buzzing around before holding notes out, not allowing a full climax. Their love of free jazz can clearly be seen as an influence on "Semen on the Mountain". The band's interplay has grown leaps and bounds, shining through with shrieking guitars on "Birth Control Blues." The band had reached a new plateau and people took notice.

In 2002, Skin Graft assembled the Oops Tour to display some of the most exciting, challenging music of the day. When it was all done, it would be discussed infamously in music circles. The Oops tour included Arab on Radar, Lightning Bolt, The Locust, Erase Eratta, Hella,

Quintron and Miss Pussycat, Wolf Eyes and The Flying Luttenbachers. The tour gave the bands a chance to meet their peers and be in a creatively supportive environment, which in turn gave them inspiration. It must have been affirming to realize there are other bands out there with similar aesthetics, taking risks with music. When the tour was over it was regarded as a great success, giving exposure to bands people might never have seen. The fact that it was a success showed that this music had a loyal fan base and was converting new fans everyday. Arab's sets on this tour were mesmerizing to watch. Craig counted off the songs in a high falsetto and the band proceeded to assault the audience unapologetically with their instruments. The singer spazzed around like a cockroach in a frying pan and the whole band seemed absorbed in their music, as if they were in another world.

"The Oops Tour was amazing, honorable, intense, scary, meaningful, and most importantly, the best tour Arab on Radar has ever been a part of. I don't think people will forget that tour too easily. I felt some very strong emotions watching all these wonderful, intelligent, talented people perform. It was a true sense of pride," remarks Schneider.

Everything seemed like it was going well until out of the blue in the fall of 2002 the band released this announcement: "Arab on Radar have officially broken up due to irreconcilable differences. Unfortunately, these differences have compromised the creative process. Arab on Radar are forever grateful to all those who have helped us out over the years." The innovative broadness of Yahweh seems to have torn the band apart. Hearing the news, Skin Graft was just as shocked as fans were about the statement. As a sort of parting gift the band compiled their scattered singles and compilation tracks for another album, The Stolen Singles, released in 2003, arguably containing some of their most accessible material.

Despite the breakup all the members continued to pursue music. Singer Eric Paul and drummer Craig Kureck joined with Richard Pelletier and Paul Vieria to form the Chinese Stars, a dance-punk band similar to AOR's early singles, but less noisy. Jeff Schneider teamed up with members of La Machine and Bossman to form Made in Mexico, which has plenty of familiar AOR distortion in it. Stephen Mattos and Pat Crump formed the duo Athletic Automaton who is known for their odd stage dress of 70s basketball uniforms and noisy, improvised songs. There seems to be no bitterness or bad blood between the band members since the breakup. They've done split singles, helped mix each other's albums, and have toured together. The band is proud of the legacy that they left behind. Stephen Mattos says fondly, "Arab on Radar always intended on creating something challenging in the music scene, right from the start. Whether directly or indirectly, we were reacting to the present state of music at the time. So we just did what we felt was in our nature to do, which was to fuck it up and confuse the hell out of people in the process. For some odd reason, many bands in Providence also wanted to fuck shit up. We just played what came out of us. I don't think there is much else I can say about it."

Chapter 1 – Wipers at the Ass Crack of Dawn

Carl Jung and his followers described "parent hunger" as the *seeking out* of the archetypal Father in the outside world, and I suppose it all started there, the inability to gain acceptance, the longing to be loved and supported. I grew up clueless. The short story, cold parents, firm but not drill sergeants. In fact, they just argued with each other, then with me when I was old enough. So much arguing, treble yelling, selfishness; of course there were good times, but not as many as there should have been. Father was insecure and stressed, he never let me do anything and when I tried, he ridiculed me and pointed out my errors, he was indifferent to my struggles and lacked the teacher's patience wholesale. Mother was a prisoner longing for her high school bubble that had burst many years ago, therefore, she'd often end up crying alone and so much evil happened when she was absent. I felt lost, no one told me the rules. I failed repeatedly and until college was a straight C student. Why try? I had to get independence and I had to prove my worth to myself; this was the fuel for the engine that drove this Red Chevy.

I didn't live too far from the school but I took that yellow bus all the same. Kids would ask the bus driver to play their cassette tapes, and of course the driver's friends' kids, the jocks, or actually the potheads in their drug-rugs, would win favor with the driver, and he'd play their shit ad infinitum. Perhaps he was buying LSD from them? Hot girls got their tracks on too: Madonna, Prince, Bruce Springsteen, Wham were the girls' choices. The lads: Bon Jovi and Crosby, Stills, and Nash. I liked Skinny Puppy. I brooded in the middle aisle seats. That was kind of my life at the time, not in the front ass-kissing or getting called out for behavioral problems, not in the back with the kids who carried knives, the unprosecuted bad people. I was a human child in the middle row, neutral but seething.

Nobody told me shit! I sincerely believed that the way these kids got their Bon Jovi tapes was that they bought blank tapes, then sat diligently by the radio, hit record/play on their boom-boxes, and recorded these tapes themselves as I did. The one time the asshole bus driver played my tape, everyone laughed. It was the first 3-4 seconds of the song cut off, clunking noises of my naïve recording effort, the last few seconds had an edit that the DJ ended out with. I remember the bus driver ejecting my tape violently and hurling it back into the mass of patchouli smelling fuck-heads I went to school with on that bus. They ripped it to shreds, tape everywhere, my work late at night, spaghetti now. Honestly it didn't affect me, I was that far gone, I just wanted to get home and fuck a sock.

Concerts would come through town and the cool kids went to them. Iron Maiden on a Friday, then on Monday all the kids had their concert shirts on. It was a badge of honor second only to some jock's football (or where I come from hockey) jersey. They had black leather spiked bracelets, I had a fluorescent yellow one... off. They had Adidas sneakers, I had an Adidas hat, Puma sneakers, I had Puma gloves, always just centimeters off. I remember wearing a Michael Jackson glove with a jean jacket with an Ozzy backpatch. I was covering all bases and striking out repeatedly.

I started hanging out with my friend Dave, a biker Harley type of dude, he had a tattoo when he was about

14 years old, a pirate, he wore a leather jacket in the summer regardless of how hot it got, I dated his sister. I used to lavish my lust for Music on Dave all to deaf ears, but he did think I had some good thoughts, sort of... He humored me, and for a very brief period I "jammed" with a neighbor of his and that guy's band. I masqueraded as a musician at this time, pretending, I was a fake, but I wanted to be one very badly. I would hop on any chance to prove I was more than some asshole in a dank bedroom doing arpeggios on a guitar in isolation. So I showed up and played. These guys were a real motley crew, some junkie drummer with a glass eye, then there was the main dude who had Down Syndrome. It was real awkward, I'd show up and hear the stories about, "hitting the guardrail on the way here," the guy was also a fucking drunk, but we'd play. We'd play this one riff, the one from The Who's "I Can't Explain," just the main riff, dun, dunna, dunt dunna, over and over, never going to a chorus or bridge of any kind, just that chugging riff over and over with the main guy soloing on bass over it. Really odd. I quit that shit after about 3 sessions. I preferred to just party with Dave and hang out. Dave and I used to take LSD and go to the Lincoln Mall. Dave had a crush on this girl named Missy who worked at the Dunkin Donuts there. He would basically stalk her. But this night we took LSD and went to sit in the booth, both drinking our hot coffee. He tried to talk to her but to no avail, as she was dating Emile (Emo) at the time so no dice. The most horrid part was that in the Dunkin Donuts there was a promotional cardboard sign, it was from the floor up a very attractive female model body in a Dunkin Donuts uniform but sexually provocatively juiced up with a mini-skirt and a

large-breasted tight shirt, but the head, the head was the "Time to Make the Donuts" guy; sexy supermodel body, then the head was a guy who looked like Luigi from *Super Mario Bros*. It sent me into a crying LSD terror, just babbling, "it doesn't make sense, it doesn't make sense." It was self-imposed MK Ultra on a micro level. We tripped in my mother's station wagon for a while, then went to see Missy, got shot down, and decided to walk around. I was fucked. We went to the Hickory Farms store and got ginger beer and brats. I still to this day love whatever that sauce was, hot mustard, maybe honey mustard?

We ventured on, now mind you, I was a truly clueless person, a naïve. There was an epic store named "Music And…" what we called Music And Dot Dot Dot. It was the first of *cool* I ever knew. A typical Mall entrance, on the left the cashier, behind a glass counter, the records and posters were up in the back up the elevated stairs on what I suppose was a mezzanine level or as I thought, a shrine. In this area I was always looking for the Holy Grail: Led Zeppelin, Metallica, and my lust, Iron Maiden. I never bought anything other than one cassette, Raven, "Faster then the Speed of Light" was the tune I was after. I had heard this on the radio, 94 HJY.

I went to every Lollapaloosa festival when that was all the rage. I idolized so many of those bands – The Ministry, Butthole Surfers, Soundgarden, Nick Cave, Beastie Boys etc. I remember walking around with my brother in the parking lot after the show and people were high and tailgating. We met this poor soul sitting on a curb in the lot, he was drinking a Corona and sitting near one of the band's vans, we thought, "wow it might be Trent Reznor," or something. The guy just got off an emotional phone call with his family/kids back in Los Angeles, he was a lighting tech, he seemed to be on the verge of overheating like a spotlight. The guy talked to us, telling us how much "the road" sucked and how he missed his family. We parted ways and he said "come back tomorrow and I'll put your name on the guest list so you can get in." We were thrilled! We dutifully gave him our full names and came back the next day. Waited in a long line to the front and we were not on the guest list. Dejected and disposed of we walked back across the quiet parking lot, we went to the wall in the back of the whole arena to see how much of a feat it would be to try to climb the wall, a few Dead-head types tried it, but over the fence was this lawn area and like football you had to sprint to the general population area to make it and those linebacker-ass security guards just picked everyone off fast, dredlocks flying everywhere. We didn't try it. Seemingly out from underneath some car or van arose some dude, he came up and said, "tickets 10 bucks" and we knew this shit was sold out months ago. But he said, "look they aren't real, but they will never know," so we bought these bootleg tickets. To our surprise they did let us in. We were noshing at the concession stand, some slush or pretzel, when this dopey guy came up to us, we said, "*Holy shit*, it's Eddie" and it was – Eddie Vedder from Pearl Jam, he leaned his head on my shoulder probably to dodge the pink-haired hoard of 15-year-old girls that were scouring the perimeter nonstop for him, or perhaps he was intoxicated. We lavished adoration on him and asked to go backstage which he declined. He was nice. We moshed the night away and sweated like only teenagers can. We imagined this carnival life was the best thing ever. We thought these bands were the most important thing in Life, this is how music seemed to me then. We stalked the crew back to the local hotel and sat in the lobby waiting for some star to walk in and lo and behold one did, Anthony Kiedis of Red Hot Chili Peppers. He had on red surfer shorts and a red Puerto Rican looking chapeau on his head. He was up checking in at the desk with his entourage; we were so ignorant we just barged in and said, "Anthony, um Anthony, Sir, could we have your autograph?" He replied, "No, I don't get into that man," in a superior droll tone. His body language was all but *fuck off*, so that is what we did, we went away and fucked off.

Chapter 2 - Hunger is the Best Sauce

"They were called "social clubs" and at that time there were more private social clubs than private housing. There were clubs on every corner and each club had it's illegal activity of card games, sport gambling, horse wagering, or neighborhood meetings to talk about and sometimes make decisions about someone who did something bad enough to get killed, like robbing someone's house, raping someone's daughter, or informing on a friend, rules that could cost a guy his life if they were broken. Of course it all depended on who broke the rules or against whom the rules were broken and who you had for friends or enemies." – Gerard "The Frenchman" Ouimette, Chapter 2 - The Hill, from "What Price Providence?"

Raymond Loreda Salvatore Patriarca Sr.

By eleventh grade my guidance counselor had had it with me. I burnt the guy out. My choices were to enlist (his advice) or drop out. These teachers had stripped my 8-period schedule back to the bare essentials, what was mandatory by law, Business Math and English; all the other 6 periods were studies. I was doing nothing, I meant nothing, I talked to no one, I wasn't even worth bullying, it was damnation by faint praise, again, banished from a tribe that I wasn't even a member of in the first place. I was the wandering, the eternal, the doorman at Pontius Pilate's estate. Luckily for me and a total surprise, my parents sent me to a private school in Providence. My first day I was dressed in a white-collared shirt all spiffy. One hour in, before classes even started, I could sense trouble. A huge kid who looked like Sean Penn walked up near me, Brent Butterworth, who ironically, according to the school listings, lived at 25 Applejack Lane in Barrington, RI., I shit you not. Brent had a huge skull ring with red ruby eyes on it and 4 or 5 huge crown spikes. He didn't say a word, he just punched my chest and held his fist stationary on me. Blood poured and pulsated out of the holes he tore in my shirt. I ran, and he just kept catching me over and over, no possible escape, learned helplessness set in, he really tried to kill me picking me up and throwing me off the curb out underneath speeding passing cars on Blackstone Boulevard. Later that day my mother picked me up in her station wagon, she had her friend with her, both ladies saw that I was upset. I took a beating. This concept no longer exists but back in the day in Providence it was what was.

A few days later a kid named Anthony Vespi asked me about Brent. Anthony didn't like me at all and didn't want to know me, but his grandfather owned a diesel truck mechanic company and my grandfather who had a well-drilling company had all his trucks and equipment worked on, inspected by his dad's place; through the grapevine his father mentioned this to him, about me going to the school, and what happened. Anthony just went up to Brent and beat his ass ruthlessly. Butterworth never fucked with me again. He held the door for me. I remember beating him up myself later in the year, slamming his head into an iron radiator in the basement stairwell over and over and over. I'm not proud of this but it had to happen. Providence had rules and it was nothing more than that.

My parents pulled me out and sent me to another Mickey Mouse school just to get some sort of placemat diploma; it was more about their pride than mine. It was at this new high school that I began to like music of the weird kind. I started going to shows, very young. It was an odd time. I cut my hair, stopped liking metal, and became "progressive" as it was called, perhaps also known as "alternative." I wore a Marilyn Monroe t-shirt; I wasn't sure what my identity was whatsoever. It was 1991. I graduated with Nicole Cianci, the mayor of Providence's daughter. For all the fucked up stuff said about her, we always got along. She drove a Volvo station wagon. I remember her getting in many accidents, once she hit an old lady's car and totaled hers. She was in a rental for a day and this really pissed her off, I remember her saying, "that stupid old bitch!" and we laughed. She was the first person I ever knew who owned a "car phone," those early cell phones that looked like a huge gray phone book. She took a call unexpectedly in our English class once, raised the antennae and started talking. The teacher said, "Um, Nicole, can you put that away please?" She retorted, "I'll have your *fucking* job!" The teacher paused timidly and just looked at the floor. I asked Nicole to join the environmental group. She rolled her eyes and said, "Dolphins are stupid," so funny; her environment was perfect, why change that shit? Her father Buddy always picked her up at school, flanked by his state trooper driver he'd come up the front stairs. He'd say, "Hey kid, hows ya doing?" and tell me tell me to say hello to my grandfather for him. At my graduation, two gay students came out whilst accepting their diplomas. Everyone was shocked at the time, the 1990s. Again, old days, old school, Buddy and my grandfather just snickered and did the old school thing. The word "faygo" was heard. I just got through it. I wanted to be making music. None of these people encouraged or understood that. When I heard years later Nicole died, I wept, she OD'd and it was a tragic life she lived. When Buddy died in 2016, Providence as I knew it died with him, it was the end of a legacy.

My family was split ethnically in two different ways. My grandfather was from the old neighborhood. He and his brother owned the first crane to work in Providence; his company laid the marble for the Statehouse or as they used to call it, "dirt mound." The marble was from a Portuguese man, Mr. Ramos, who lived down the street from my parents. My great uncle Anthony was a connected guy. He had a union job, stayed home, not much to do then. His crew built the Jamestown Bridge, he had the contract, the company used their cranes to move all kinds of shit. I remember him telling me about guys who had to go "bye bye" back in the day. They had the sea wall pushing back all the water and day in day out they were pouring concrete into this vast shaft to build the pylons for the bridge. Somebody said something back in those days, they took a dip, *plop*, nobody heard another thing out of them again. Who knows how many stiffs are built into that bridge? Call the Samaritans, fuck, call the Romans. There are so many stacked in that bridge! My Uncle Anthony, eventually, tragically, and to no fault of his own, accidentally ran into an old gommada over on the Hill. She was eighty and he pulled out of a parking spot in his huge black Lincoln and ran her over, he just wasn't looking, that's all. Bam, dead. She was an aunt of somebody everybody knew. The old man Raymond Patriarca sanctioned him. Patriarca ran most business from what the locals called "garlic mountain," which is more famously known as the Federal Hill area of Providence, as it stands today. There was a code of ethics that we all knew, being from Providence. Nothing happened in this city, in bars, on the street, and in all the music clubs, without the blessing of this man, nothing. This is what we grew up understanding and no one said a word about it, that was for sure.

My Uncle Anthony never worked or profited again. He ended up depressed and all he did that ever amounted to anything after that was to take care of my great grandmother, who lived to be 101 years old; she never put salt on anything, ever. She was in this nursing home and my uncle thought someone who worked there, a Haitian guy, was stealing her clothes and her rose-scented hand lotion. He freaked out one day and wrapped the cord from the window blind around this guy's neck and choked him out, screaming profanities in Italian. He wasn't allowed to see her anymore; the family was sick of his goombah shit and disowned him. He died alone and was cremated; no one went to his funeral. My family had lost a lot of pride and I feel like this was why I may have had something to prove later on, when it came to the music.

My grandmother married one of the chosen ones, high up in the hierarchy of a certain persuasion. He told me "never marry an Italian" amidst one of their fights; he thought she was too needy and dramatic. Her cooking was excellent. I remember her pride. One day when I was very young we stopped at a yard sale, there was an old cigar box on one of the tables, amongst junk jewelry and vintage Pez dispensers, and I opened it. Inside was a switch-blade knife. As a young boy this was titillating. When I went to touch it the owner yelled at me saying, "Shut that box! You don't touch that!" and I ran to the car crying. As we began to drive away I told my grandfather and he sided with the guy; my grandmother (being Italian) freaked out and she went back and yelled at the guy in Italian. She got in the car and said, "You can touch whatever you like, you are a ... Schneider." I knew she wished a different last name came out. But that is the thing, once your family speaks English it is over, your culture is gone, nothing to keep people in line, no religion, you get McReligion, so language, culture, fall away, you get destroyed. Now you come from nowhere, you cut down the trees, cleared the lot, you speak English and your roots are dead. To me Italians and then the Serbians and Russians who took over a lot of it died the same way, "*our thing*" can't even be spoken in English. This is what people don't understand, I think this is why trying to make that band something to identify with, a crew, not to be fucked with, it was an effort to replant some trees in our neighborhood.

Chapter 3 – Histamine Scampi

After all this shit, I had to get out on my own, totally. Two weeks after graduating high school I abruptly announced I was leaving. They didn't give two shits. My mother once said one simple phrase of advice, she said, "Jeffrey, whatever you do, just don't be yourself." How could I, when there never was a self, none was built? With nothing left to lose when I was 17 I impulsively moved with a friend to Seattle, Washington, not a good place for a depressed person. This is why they drink so much fucking coffee. I stepped off the plane and went directly to the Capitol Hill neighborhood, the local hip zone in 1991, I wanted to feel out the band scene, buy some CDs... Out of a garbage strewn alley a banshee tackled me on the ground into the bar chowder below. Fighting for my life, this 300 lb. insanely intoxicated Native American was on top of me, mounting me like an MMA fighter. I clawed him, he shrieked, and rolled off me cackling psychotically. His spit went into my eyes and mouth; toothless wine juice. I got up, scared as fuck and walked on, welcome? This shit just got worse. Working in a sweatshop. It was me, my roommate I moved out there with, and about 200 Chinese slaves whose visas were being held to keep them abusively controlled. They would line up at the bubbler during the break and got nothing but water, the other two of us stood in line at the vast spread of all sorts of cafeteria shit; they didn't even think of catering to their cultural foods, those assholes. Outside on the streets, after work, I was being insulted repeatedly by musicians when I was aspiring to join the next Nirvana. In truth there never was a Seattle music scene, it is a myth, the whole "grunge" thing was made up, there were movies about it, and coffee shops, but it was all a Potemkin Village. There were crust punks who told me to, "just listen to the Ramones," so I did. It was all over here and really it never was here.

I came home to my roommate (the guy who I moved out there with) junkie-fucking in my bed, which was no more than a 5-foot closet in an open 1-room dwelling. I am six feet two inches tall, which made things awkward. His street-punk girl took out a wad of MacDonald's napkins and crammed them in between her legs, telling me the virtues of "McPads" and how she was "raggin'." They fixed together, in front of me, which was repulsive and disturbing. I took my last $500 and caught a red-eye back home. My parents wouldn't let me stay so I began couch surfing in Providence. I was homeless for a while, for about a week, okay. I slept outside because it was July. Slept in Kennedy Plaza in downtown Providence on a bench one night. I assimilated with the fuckin' bums. That was a personal low.

I listen to 1964 Bob Dylan's "The Lonesome Death of Hattie Carroll" and wonder, how did this imp write such music? Then I admire, that this person is probably tortured by the fact that no one could possibly understand how he did it, or what has happened to him since he did it, no one cares about him, even though he did do it. This shit should be taken as it was then and not now, and the importance then is not what it is now. The stories that follow, I sincerely hope are met with happiness and joy, with the connection of reason and emotion, with the power of wisdom behind them. I hope it saves some from grave mistakes and encourages others to be wild and bold, restraining nothing, being you and loving you and reaching out with the voice and wisdom of youth, passion and honor. Go forth with this as an offering, go forth with this as a farewell, go forth with this as the embryo for what is yet to come.

I had been taking guitar lessons during high school on and off from this really cool guy named Greg, he looked a lot like Jimi Hendrix, he had big hair, but being black in the 1980's was tough hair-wise, he couldn't get Steve Perry hair either, this we had in common. He lived near my school and I'd walk up there and he'd give me lessons; nobody really cared to know where I was going or what I did, so why not? He was such a great guy, another father figure, who would teach me theory (the boring shit) but simultaneously, to keep my attention, he'd say, "Okay man, here is how to play War Pigs", with the two finger chords. Greg was such a great teacher and I owe a lot to him musically, he probably would be sad to see what I made with it, but hell, I tried, and he tried to help me. His mom was very cool and would just show me the door down to Greg's bachelor pad room in the basement. I could tell so many girls adored him, he was getting laid often, sometimes the lesson would abruptly end when a really hot girl came down the stairs, he'd just politely ask me to go home, like right now. I was confused, but I really thought of Greg as a hero so just being invited over was the highlight of my life at the time. He had a sweet set up, carpet on the walls in his room. We used to smoke pot, and get his kitten really high by proxy, man, that cat would run around those walls like a NASCAR track, it would go from floor to ceiling, around and around, just manic, it was funny. He sold me his guitar, this hot pink

Ibanez guitar from the 80's, he was done with, I put on it a matching hot pink Andre the Giant sticker and bought a hot pink locking guitar strap. I played a Marshall JCM-900 Half-stack at the time, I thought it was a hot rig for a week or two there... Famed poster artist/activist/RISD grad Shep Fairey (that pimp) had a loft in Providence and to get all of his work done he'd let locals, street urchins, mostly us wanna-be skater types come up and cut stickers with him in exchange for some stickers or other art, but I digress.

My brother and I had been playing music together. We would place advertisements in the local rag, ours was called *The Providence Phoenix*, a go-to paper that had show listings and classified sections. Our ad stated, "Looking for vocals and drums, influences include: The Beatles, The Ramones and The Stooges." There were many odd responses. We loaded this gear down a bulkhead basement in these two kids' house in Cumberland, RI, two brothers also. Right away the vibe was off; apparently they were very, very excited and had their loving parents' full support of their "band" Lung Mustard. The parents were right there cackling and showering supportive comments, helping us with gear, asking about our background, our last name extensively. They gave all these suggestions, we were all coming from the same tar pit, only these poor bastards were so much more deep in it. The father wanted the schmaltz, "Give it to me like Baby Driver!" he kept howling. We literally were like a bridge over troubled water. "The schmaltz! The schmaltz!" he kept encouraging. Of course our riffs were the most satanic sounding depressed bullshit one could muster, but regardless our cheering squad wanted, "Give me that Cecilia! C'mon boys." It was heinous. My brother and I were scarred enough as it was, this reenactment of *The Graduate* soundtrack wasn't really what we needed at this point in our lives. It was as if we alone had to carry the flag of Israel to conquer the Egyptian Army with our music. These guys missed the tips of their cocks far more than we did; we just wanted to play music and there was no problem with just playing, doing a good job and hey, keep the tip. This had totally different meaning for these guys. The father wanted to book studio time for us because Lung Mustard was going places. He probed with a shluchim speech and I was bullied into revealing my ambitions for someday going to Berklee School of Music, he went on a rant about the musicians in Paul Simon's band on *Graceland* and how many were graduates of Berklee. It was discouraging. We didn't even have our gear plugged in yet. We played a few horrid songs, Feel Like Makin' Love, Freebird, Simple Man. We played "Eighteen" by Alice Cooper, which only made the situation worse. We felt weird in this basement so we started to break down our shit. The father and the two sons said, "no, no, no, just leave your gear here, come back, come baaack!" We humbly declined but from every angle it just escalated. "You do want to record don't you? Where you going? This is your best opportunity in life, there will never be another for you. Paul Simon was 4' 9'' and bald at age 21, that didn't stop him from making it!" They pressured on and on. We bailed the fuck out fast, I left a guitar cable behind, and in my broke-ass existence at the time this was a big deal. The Six-Hour War was over, so sorry, I am a rock, I am an island…

Later that week we got a call from Eric Paul (not his name at the time). He was interested in the Stooges reference in our ad and wanted to meet up. My brother wasn't very interested. When we agreed to meet in the Stop and Shop parking lot in North Smithfield, RI, I went alone. I looked like a hillbilly mind you. Eric was there with his girlfriend Jen in this little Toyota, I think it was blue. They both got out to chat, it was obvious they were much more hip than I was, she looked like *Rosemary's Baby* era Mia Farrow, he looked like Perry Farrell of Jane's Addiction, long leather jacket, greasy hair, earrings, I swear he had some weird ascot on. We talked and he told me he had been playing with Steve who was in a band and that Steve had considered jamming with me one time to see what was what. Steve knew Andrea and she had friends who had a practice space in Providence that on an off night they said we could use. Eric wanted only me, not my brother to come, which was a rift between my brother and me for a while (he dodged a bullet honestly). I went to this cavernous space in what was called the Vingi Building, a mill run by local mafioso family across the street from the post office in Providence. On the ground level it was a fruit distribution center, big trucks, loading docks, all sorts of daily hustling and bustling getting the fruit out to local Italian restaurants, but at night only shady criminal shit happened over there. We humped my shit up to the 3rd floor (no elevator) and set up. It was G_d-awful cacophony and I think Steve thought I was a total waste of time, especially showing up with that fucking hot pink Ibanez with the hot pink Andre sticker on it. We played a few more times just the 3 of us; Steve announced that Andrea wanted to be in a band and agreed to come and "just play bass a bit" with us, probably the idea was to get in the space and someday play with the other bands that practiced in there, she was jamming with them too. The Alley Cats, an all-girl band, and 59 Teeth, an older dude band we were scared of. There was this caste system back then, impenetrable. She was way cooler than us. Eric got this dude Jamie, a guy he went to college with or something. Jamie was a jazz drummer, very quiet dude, he was Chinese, I think, all I know is he played odd glockenspiels and shit... We asked him to just play straight 4/4 beats which seemed to annoy him, he was always watching his wristwatch, we just pissed him off. Very generously Steve had 2 Gibson Les Paul guitars and he bluntly said, "the guitar you have sucks, just play mine so we can try to do something." I heartily agreed and it felt great to play a real guitar; I eventually bought it off of Steve.

We had a very large practice space at the Vingi Building. It housed over 20 other practice spaces, all varying in size. It was not uncommon to bump into other musicians in the hallways. On the second floor (we were on the third) was the Hell's Angels bar, and a strange character named Henry. Henry lived in his space, believe it or not, without utilities, heat, or a shower. His lifelong preoccupation was his "work" making metal jewelry, skull necklaces, and some badass Metallica bootleg necklace shit. Acrid fumes emanated from his doorway and we always joked about the incredible amount of chromosome damage that must have occurred being in that space 24/7, we could hear brain cells popping as we walked by his door like fuckin' popcorn. Henry always wanted to hang out, he'd knock on our door while we were playing and try to set up tentative plans to, "get wicked high, like in Space, high as shit with me later, I got some great stuff, I'll sell you some." His eyes would cross when he was really up to something. We'd make vague plans but would play for 4 more hours forgetting his surprise visit. We'd leave and tippy toe by his door saying, "shit, do you think he's still awake in there?" Whispered to pass by, but he'd always holler, with pressured speech, "I *AM NOT* sleeping! I'm just waiting for you guys with the lights off, my eyes hurt." Then we'd have to hang out. We almost always declined, we felt bad, but there were times when he caught us on the way out, of course it was after 4-5 hours of practice and we were worn out, so vulnerable. He'd scuttlebutt us on the way out and welcome us into his toxic domain. I remember he had his driver's license nailed to the wall, amongst hundreds of other seemingly personal documents wallpapered up there, he looked much saner in that picture. He'd always try selling us speed and homemade meth, I imagine the bikers were his suppliers. It was always a real pain in the ass to load our equipment into this space as it had no elevator. Lucky for us we only played 2-3 shows during these first 4 agoraphobic years of existence. I do recall one time, very late at night, perhaps early morning after a show, Henry showed up at the top of the sprawling mill building stairs, his head half-shaved, like the right side of his whole head was shaved, bleeding that dull-razor blood, spotty; he was tweaking hard, blood stains on his right shoulder, out in the Cosmos somewhere. He was very adamant about loading our gear in, helping us, he thought he was Christ. We just let him. He picked up Andrea's 6-speaker Traynor bass cabinet on his shoulder (left) and with super-ape strength he carried it up all

those stairs. He was ranting about the Anti-Christ,
barking at the moon. This was normal at this time.

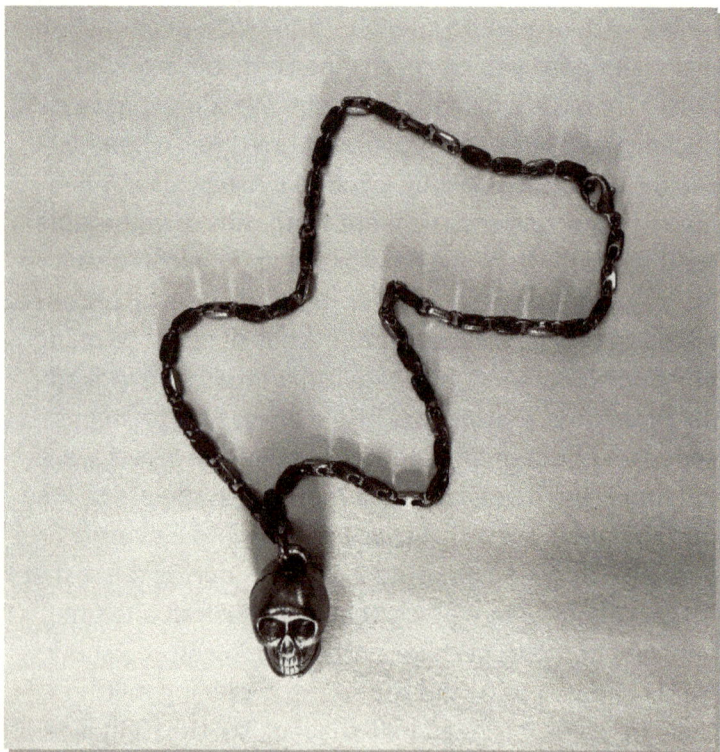

Chapter 4 – Well-Drinking and Well-Drilling

We worshipped the band Six Finger Satellite. They were signed to Sub Pop Records, which was the world to us at this time. The very first contact I had with this band was on December 11, 1991, it was at a show with Jesus Lizard, Six Finger Satellite and Glazed Baby. The "indie" underground was in full swing and labels such as Sub Pop, Touch and Go, and Mute were the colonists of the musical landscape. I would go, religiously, to any Sub Pop show and to their credit, they had superior marketing strategies, their "Single of the Month Club" had me addicted. The shows were "showcases" all for Sub Pop bands quite often, all focused on the label, I remember later on seeing Six Finger Satellite, Lumpano, and Hardship Post, a horrid musical match, but nonetheless Sub Pop Records.

These were the days of Sick of it All, Buffalo Tom, Jawbox, Girls Against Boys, Urge Overkill, Fugazi, Polvo, on and on, this was the context. Six Finger Satellite was a tier above all of these bands, musically, stylistically and innovatively. I saw them again at Club Babyhead in Providence, Rhode Island. It was Green Magnet School, Six Finger Satellite, and Dungbeetle. This was one of those iconic shows, one you are never the same after. The singer of Dungbeetle (a short-lived, local, amazing band) was Sam Lipsyte, who is now a well-established author/professor in New York; at the time Sam was a maniac. He looked exactly like Bluto from Animal House, a rotund sweaty boor of a man, he wore a wrestling belt and did intimate moves on stage; at times he just touched people's faces very uncomfortably while performing. Dungbeetle really shredded and I had never seen anything like it before. Rewinding, I must say, Six Finger Satellite was also mind-bogglingly good. I forget if it was this show or another around this time, but they wore letterman sweaters, the look was Coll*ege* (as in Mondos vs. Coll*eges*, the Rhode Island version of Greasers and Squares from the 1950's). The drummer Rick Pelletier and bassist Chris Dixon took the stage first, setting up the backbeat for their song "Deadpan," off of the album *The Pigeon is the Most Popular Bird*. Right on the note the two guitarists, John Maclean and Pete Phillips came onstage and landed perfectly into the opening synchronized guitar riffs, J. Ryan came out last in an epic way barking out the vocals, it was fucking stellar. I wanted to do whatever it was they were doing, unorthodox and powerful music with intellect. I didn't know what I was getting myself into.

Eric had an "in" with the Ryan brothers, J. (Jeremiah) Ryan and John "Von" Ryan. I am not perfectly clear of the details but they all came from the same town, Lincoln or Cumberland, RI, that region of the state; they had the same coach on the baseball teams in middle school, they had childhood connections. One source of envy was that in the very early 1990s J. Ryan gave Eric a mixed tape and encouraged good music with him. It was all the sacred hits one needs to know: The Stooges, Captain Beefheart and his Magic Band, The Birthday Party, Chrome, Come, Tubeway Army, Can, The Scientists, Big Black, Butthole Surfers, Mule, Thee Headcoats, Devo, Pere Ubu's "30 Seconds over Tokyo." I remember vividly being envious of that, not because I wanted a tape, but because J. was always cold to me, he thought I was a no talent loser and at the time I was one.

The funny thing was that Eric being so close to J.

Ryan made it hard, if not impossible, for him to befriend John Maclean the guitarist and main songwriter for Six Finger Satellite because those guys were like Pete Towshend and Roger Daltrey, fire and ice at this time. I started to get to know Maclean through Andrea, all of us young-uns borrowed his records wantonly whether he knew it or not, she just loaned them to us, which was awesome. I developed a beneficial alliance with John Maclean, we both helped each other with long term strategies which inflicted costs on other members of this musical population. But we never really got along. He didn't speak much at all; we'd sit in awkward silence and he was kind of an uncomfortable person to be around. He spoke in puffs, groans, and whimpers. I could see how he sort of manipulated people to get his way, but he was never outwardly demanding of anything from anyone. He just made you do his dirty work for him. He was a master at this technique.

Time went on in this developmental stage. Every time Andrea was around John Maclean, the animus was apparent. They were old war buddies, former lovers, checking in on sobriety, AA lingo used, but the hurt was there, this ship had sailed. "Me I Disconnect From You" by Tubeway Army was one of her favorite songs I remember her saying at this time, go figure... Out of respect, I don't want to get into the details, but she incurred all sorts of problems from this guy, health and otherwise. I'm surprised she didn't just *kill* him, honestly.

Maclean was a mentor of sorts, he had a magnetism to him that is for sure. He was part of the Providence College survivor's group: J. Ryan, him, Guy Benoit, Ben McOsker, a few others. Real Catholic shit, that repressive environment really led to excess in other evil ways; they were the satanic choirboys. I recall a story about Maclean being really high on heroin, he was real deep into addiction, shooting with toilet water the whole 9 yards, he nodded out in a hotel room and awoke to a prostitute he'd been fixing with sucking him off, he realized it was a tranny, and the story goes, he said, "who cares, just keep going" and flopped back into the bed, into the realm of *Naked Lunch*. The fact that Maclean jokes about his addiction in interviews in the music press made me cringe, but it was such a part of his identity, he had a tattoo of a heroin needle on his arm, like a target, very big fat needle right over where you would inject, it was creepy. I am sure he probably lived through some really traumatic stuff. Fucking Catholics...

Ironically, working at Bread and Circus, a health food store, was how I met J. Ryan (Seafood Counter) and John Maclean (Deli). I was the salad bar supervisor (of the salad bar, not coworkers, it was a job of one.) This woman who fled the Iraq War from Kuwait named Randa used to call J. Ryan "Mr. Shark," which was a perfect way to sum up his personality. Bread and Circus at the time was pretty okay, they would allow musicians to take time off then return to their jobs, it was ideal place to work. I ended up quitting Bread and Circus in order to focus on music as a half-baked career. The hot shit in Providence at this time was a band from Ivy League colleges named Les Savvy Fav. No one liked these guys besides those in the elite; they never assimilated, they were distractions to our scene. These Favs were pompous but through some keyboard alliance they won the favor of the Six Finger Satellite guys. Their music for the most part was aimed at sexually harassing art school freshmen. Weak, soulless songs... They did the chameleon: whatever music was "in" that week, they adapted to. Ultimately they did the "Art School Migration to NYC" and exploited much that was good about Providence, claiming it as their own. David Byrne was their G_d and his methods are well studied by rich kids like this. It was never genuine and their music is unmemorable and meaningless. These people are meaningless.

I don't even know what to say about all of this music at this time, it was confusing. It definitely jolted me right to the fucking brain, but I have no concept of how much it warped or in exactly which way it shaped me. It changed my overall outlook of life, challenged all preconceived notions of how to play music, how to play guitar, using riffs over chords, it showed me how to breathe in Music confidently. I found worth here, self-worth; when no one supports you, you must set goals if for no other reason than to have facts of your own successes, this way it doesn't matter what others say or do, support or otherwise, about your creations, about you. There were times I thought I was listening to G_d speaking with us personally through this music, sending a signal, telling us what to do. We operated so deep in the underground, at the bottom. If someone in the mainstream even mentioned things like "Sonic Youth" or "Big Black," in an interview in the mainstream press we were really excited.

THEME TO A B/W MOVIE

YELLOW SHOT SISTER

William Tell

GROWN

SCISSORS + GLUE

Jamie's last show

Chapter 5 – 'Twas A Frosty Christmas Eve

Time went by, I now was living on Hope St. near the area they called Fox Point in Providence, RI.   Sad times. Well-drilling, breaking my back all fucking day and drinking 1 pint of vodka per night, it was a shitty lifestyle. I had this crazy landlord Moshe Gerber, he kept threatening me with his AK-47; he was an Israeli thug and spoke broken English. He still owes me 400 bucks that fuck, total slumlord, my father would argue with him in a patronizing tone about the squalid conditions of the property, "Now Moshe, my son has to live here, Moshe..." It was a mess. Close quarters, I had this L.L. Bean-ish type of upstairs neighbor; she was always fucking at top of her lungs, real athletic, she was 19 years old, a Brown University freshman, the guy she hypersonically fornicated with was a professor at Brown. He was about 50, he really looked the part of a pedophile, those glasses, the type of twat that reads Jonathan Franzen proudly in public, the original man spreader. The professor and I in passing used to stare each other down, eye to eye contact, he knew what I was doing, smoking my pot, and I knew exactly what he up to, every last sweaty groan of it.

Our social lives outside of playing music were real difficult. I recall a Christmas that was unholy. I was going to my parents' house for three days. Eric was staying at my apartment over the holiday; the poor guy had no one, no family. I had this cat, Harold (female), who he had agreed to care for. I must have been incredibly messed up. I'd drink that vodka, perhaps a bottle every other night or three. It was a low place to find myself, I smoked a lot of pot at this time. For some reason I felt guilty for the bastard, the cat that is. My girlfriend and I were going to leave for our trip but beforehand I decided, whilst very high, to give Harold three whole cans of wet cat food, then I added a ring of milk, because she loved to drink milk, it was a treat. To top it off I sprinkled on top a dusting of catnip. It was a feline's dream sundae, a McFlurry for fuzzy. I may have actually put a cherry on top. Of course poor Harold, as any cat would, spitefully gobbled down the entire dessert in about five minutes of me leaving. Eric told me when I got back she bazooka-barfed so bad the odor was horrid; after this he had to put her outside, he claimed. I was wicked pissed to come home to, luckily, find her outside the door. It was all fucked up, I feel bad for everyone involved. R.I.P. Harold.

      With our abundance of riffs and rifflers, in that practice space at the Vingi Building, we carved out a corner for ourselves. These days, G_d, we had so much time on our hands. Eric was a thrift store maniac and always was shopping around at various Salvation Army stores (Sally's Boutique). For some reason he purchased about 20 or 25 umbrellas. We spent a few hours on a tall ladder with some fishing line hanging these all from the rafters in the space. I can't remember if we did that first, then called the band Umbrella or vice versa. It was just that simple, the band name Umbrella, it was okay, we sat with it, but never really felt like the name possessed the chutzpah we would have down the road, but at this time it was perfect for who we were, what we played, and how confident we were. We were not that solid as a band; John Von was kind of a hired gun, he agreed to play drums with us, he was disconnected, had other things to do, he was in many bands before, Von

Ryan's Express (with Dan St. Jacques) being the best of them. He was checked out and aloof but who could blame him? Umbrella - it kept us dry, happy in our practice space, and it worked out as a band name for a while.

Our musical education progressed. Some great shit was happening at the time, we all went to see Shellac for the first time, at this Polish Club, last minute info that the show was happening, they would DiY it the whole way, great gear, their own PA, they would bypass all Clear Channel venues or corporate clubs (a big musical-political issue at the time). I remember being blown away by it all. Seeing the band Codeine, again smoked by them, just because it was so, so slow, but it was professional and I could tell it was cool. Seeing Jesus Lizard at Lupo's Heartbreak Hotel was amazing, David Yow climbed up this narrow drain, probably 1-inch thick, an air conditioning drain, all the way to the ceiling. He wore these long johns and no shirt, during the show he pulled the long johns up over his head, he looked like a psychotic frog, it was the best. There was another Jesus Lizard show about a year later and all I can recall is being thrown out on to the street by the bouncer of Lupo's, a guy who ironically was in a band with my wife's parents in the 1970s, he hated me, these were some highlights of the low points of my life at this time. Like an Assyrian, he opened the back door of the club using my head as a battering ram. We learned a lot about Music business in these 9th Century BC times.

Speaking historically, there was a superstition about this ancient water fountain on Benefit Street in the heart of RISD campus, near where all of the Edgar Allen Poe folklore went down. If you drank from this fountain then you would never leave Providence, we all ended up drinking from the old crusty fountain, quite a commitment; it was rather slimy water. Honestly, my fondest memories are those of our close friends at the time. I must sincerely give props to Jen and Renee, and all the others who believed in us at this time, the friends who sat through so many shows, told us we should go on, encouraged this toddler-phase maelstrom, put us in time out and praised us when we did good, those who supported us financially and emotionally. I often wonder, in the thick of all this, would I have stayed with anyone or any band who had such a demanding interest? One that never paid off? One that required such stress, so much air sucked out of the room? Probably not, but they did. Jen and Renee were with us through thick and thin and we didn't deserve them. Late nights early on were trying. So often the thought arrives, "Why the fuck am I doing this?" late, in that darkness. They were there to keep the light on. We had so much fun together, we went everywhere together, all of us back then. They saw idiocy, persistent idiocy play out, and probably our best shows ever. Thank you from the bottom of my heart. Some call it superstition, others, faith, and we all ended up drinking from the fountain.

Craig was Eric's friend and had just finished film school at Emerson. He was a bass player but we already had one. We did jam with him once at this time but some back room conversation ensued between him and Eric, whatever they discussed prevented us from pursuing the project further, for his sake not ours. Regardless, Craig used to come to every one of Umbrella's shows; he videotaped a lot of the early gigs we did. We all were one big crew back then, aimlessly trying to find our way forward creatively.

We were milling around our practice space, where we practically lived these days; we spent so much time there. In came one of the other bands who we shared the space with, The Alley Cats. They were puzzled by our habits, one of them said, "Hey, do you guys have any shows lined up?" a typical band topic of conversation. The thought really had never dawned on us, this is how clueless we were, so we were like, "No, not, um, really…" She said there were a few shows at Club Babyhead that they could not play, but the venue was looking for another band, and if we wanted to we could do it. We autistically agreed. It was awkward because we hadn't a clue how to do a show ourselves. We'd seen many but they were all objectified and idealized, the nuts and bolts of how to do it were beyond our mechanics at this time. Andrea knew the booking agent and the owner of Club Babyhead, Jeff, pretty well through the older kids' scene she was a part of and that we had missed. We ended up getting on a lot of great shows: Ween, who were very stoned on pot and threw their rider's worth of vegetable plates up over the wall that separated out dressing rooms on top of our heads. Branch Manager, who was on Fugazi's label Dischord, how could they suck? We thought, like-sounding bands, like-minds, like-music; it wasn't, it was a fucking heinous crap-pile. They certainly did not run home to D.C. and tell Ian MacKaye how awesome we were and to call us based on our show, like we thought they would. No Black Flag romanticism for us, sorry Henry, we failed, we mustn't have weight-lifted enough. A few other local gigs were had. We went out to shows once or twice a week, we lived music at this time, worked and practiced and went out to shows all the time.

The music scene in Providence was hard to describe at this time. There were no weird bands, very few even punk rock bands going on, people were catching their breath from the 1980s still, and no inhalers were convincing them to try "crazy shit" again, so things were safe and rather sterile. Big acts like Urge Overkill and The Pixies, Fugazi and the whole 3rd wave Ska revival wretch that I fucking refuse to get into here or anywhere else for that matter. Not much weird stuff, what we called CPR (crazy punk rock) was going on. A local rock-a-billy gang, who sarcastically, you better not fuck with, named "The Stilettos" were always gooning around town, these sick-a-billy idiots took themselves so seriously, dressing in all sorts of pompadorian Hairspray sort of ways. Now I think they are a kickball team, quite a demotion. There were always designated locals who peripherally knew some of these big acts, so look out, here comes Johnny Two-Tone who knows Maynard from Tool and you better roll out the red carpet for Johnny, this kind of shit... It was not high school, far from it, but there were tones, definite tones; these were the machismo days and I hated it.

Somehow Andrea, through knowing the Mafia-Vatican-Pimp-#1 posse, got us on Load Records compilation *A Bitter Pill to Swallow*, a great compilation of Providence's best and brightest bands at the time. Umbrella's song "Crown" debuts on that comp. I think John Maclean recorded that for us, some sort of ex-girlfriend guilt motive, making amends perhaps, Step work. Ben McOsker was and has always been on the scene in all of its iterations, the guy loves music, he really is a pillar of the Providence Music Scene and did more to promote it and help it than anyone I can remember. He can suck his own dick, no lie, as evidenced by the cover of the Landed "Dairy For Dinner" 7-inch he put out, so I won't keep lavishing praise, but it is all true; he helped in big and small ways. The guy gave me my first turntable when I began record collecting, it was these fatherly acts I will always remember, like teaching a son how to fish, it was taken that way.

We played this one posh art venue called the Rouge Gallery; the owner, a guy named Jim Draper, helped us along the way. Jim resembled Paul Schaffer of David Letterman Show fame, bald, weird, he really liked Andrea a lot, perhaps too much. He did sort of purposely put us on some sour gigs, ones he knew were with people we had beef with; perhaps he was trying to be Andy Warhol, a Napoleon in rags and the language that he used? I recall getting assaulted by this guy Nick from the band Thee Hydrogen Terrors. We played that night with women's stockings on our heads, pantyhose, which was ripped off of Devo, even though we didn't know that. This little prick, in a cocaine rage I assume, threw a metal folding chair at us, they hated us, these local bands like Thee Royal Crowns, Ashley Von Hurter and the Haters, Boss Fuel, especially Medicine Ball, the band that contained this guy who worked at the local hip record store called In Your Ear; his name was Mark Stone, he was obsessed with *rating* your purchases, being a total unabashed critic was his modus operandi especially to us young people. He loved The Stranglers which by and large considering the canon of their music, fucking suck; Medicine Ball was a long boring set to get through too, we just dreaded it. Guy Benoit, the singer of Thee Hydrogen Terrors was also dissing us hard in the local press and in person. I think Guy just got wrapped up in the present moment and didn't read the wind shift very well, instead of dancing with the change he wrestled with it. Lots of people at the time in this scene went the confrontation route and didn't roll with resistance, change scared them; they were conservatives. It came to a head in many situations at the bar. Many people dropped out of the club scene to play at the loft spaces, it got fierce. The Rockers vs Artfags War had begun.

Chapter 6 – Borscht Belt Blues

The first time I met JWD or John Dwyer, "Dwyer," as he was known to us, he was a bike messenger/weed dealer local who shared an apartment with Steve and this guy Will from the band White Mice. Dwyer called Will "Will-My-Crack-In" which really pissed him off. Dwyer was no foreigner to sarcasm, I'm not going to psychoanalyze this shit, but I will say his life led him to know how to hit first as to not get hit first. He had a stately jaw, quick wit, and could operate coolly when greened out in major cosmic THC-ulation. He always came in in a rush, manic a bit, but John was always really funny, a natural entertainer. I remember being really insecure about my visual art, my paintings, I once painted this portrait, kind of a dred-locked gent, a Perry Farrell type of scarecrow, and Steve looked at it and we both laughed because he said "Dwyer" at the same time I did in synchronicity.

Their apartment was another place we hung out at frequently. We had a motley crew at the time; there were these two guys, Larry Marshall and his tag along buddy Vin. Vin was really out there, nice guy, but he was impaired by life. All the shows we were doing early on at Lupo's Heartbreak Hotel and the Met Café, these were mostly what they'd call "showcase" shows, meaning someone booked them to appeal to a wide audience of college students, in a bar setting, perhaps 4 bands per night, starting at 9 pm and ending at 1 am, typically. We would invite Vin to do a brief introduction of us like Jerry Lewis's scene, MC's, perhaps tell a joke or two. His brain went abnormally haywire and over time this persona of Vin took him over. It was a bizarre act that blossomed into a musical opera of sorts. I recall sitting at Steve's once while Larry and Vin were there. Larry convinced us to allow Vin a captive audience to dry-run his next performance; after bong hits galore we obliged. Steve, Will, Larry Marshall, and I sat on the couch, the lighting had to be low. Vin came out in a graduation gown, an academic mortarboard, he had this Alice Cooper-esque eye make up on, but not black, blood red, very scary. On one arm he had a locked handcuff draping from his wrist, this looked to be legitimately bloody for some reason, who the hell knew what he was doing or was going to do. Like a Muslim calling to prayer in Saudi Arabia, he started chanting and singing all sorts of weird disturbing shit. He began singing (still to this day an awesome song) "Tender Tara," an ode to Craig's very sexy girlfriend at the time, Tara. It was odd, lines about "just wanting to bathe her" and stuff, it got real strange in the parts, he sang in a high pitched child voice which made it even more psychologically intense. Freudian garble mixed with a murderous tone. We were pinned to the back of the couch as he traipsed around, obviously in an extreme state of mind. In the middle of all this the light flicked on and Dwyer barged in, going, "What the fuck is happening here?" laughing. Vin got a bit miffed and focused his energy towards Dwyer who ran back into his room shrieking half-jokingly like a scream track queen. Then it was over, silence fell, Vin was consoled by Larry, Vin was breathing heavily; we had all been through enough that night.

With a heavy heart I think back about Larry Marshall; he was our best friend. Eric really took a liking to vulnerable folks and Larry was one. He had such a rough life living off the social system due to disabilities, public busses, subsidized housing, all the hell of poverty and neglect, this poor guy endured. Shame on every Providence politician who caused this, you failures, you crooks, you maintained this violent city and allowed it all, sipping your wine on vacations in Naples, fuck you. Apologies, I digress, we always stood up for Larry and he was a close, loving comrade. Every once in a while Larry would have a show and we would provide the backing band, whoever was around, Larry Marshall and the Sharpshooters. Steve was most involved with these gigs; he seemed to be the most official Sharpshooter. These times were great, we often rehearsed last second or not at all, we'd do our best to keep up with whatever direction Larry wanted to go in, playing harmonica or fiddles, stuff you'd never think of doing. My girlfriend who was not a musician at all hopped in one night, it was fun all around. Years later, sadly, after we had gone up the ladder of bullshit, we lost touch with him. Larry had fallen into homelessness, which was his choice, but the few times I'd drive by and see him out late at night, I'd pull over to talk to him and he would run away. I'd see him by day and he was very paranoid, mental illness had taken over. There were serious efforts to help him but the damage was done. I heard bad stories from friends about meathead college fucks assaulting him late at night after the bars let out. I hope whoever the people are that did that shit rot in fucking hell forever.

Owner Ben McOsker put an early Arab On Radar song on another Load Records compilation *Repopulation Program*. There was some glimmer of hope. It was again a documentation of a certain time in Providence Music history, if you weren't on that comp, then you really didn't matter in the town at the time. If you listen to it entirely, it didn't matter if you didn't matter, honestly.

We tried to sell these comp CD's at the silly shows we were playing at the time, but not much was happening.

Around this time we played an interesting gig at The Living Room with The Dictators. It was bleak, no one came, we sucked, Il Duce just sat out on the loading dock. I kept thinking that here sits the guy who Courtney Love hired to kill Kurt Cobain, right there, wow... These were the type of shows we sought out at the time and the milieu we thought we somehow belonged to, The Murder Junkies or some other musical degeneracy. All in all, these shows were meaningless, a light fart in a heavy wind.

Eric was in Florida on vacation and he wrote me passionately about Marilyn Manson, this pervert band he saw when he was down there. He was excited reporting how the singer had this couch on stage and would molest his underage fans on it the whole show; he stuck dildos up his butthole at this time. Marilyn Manson was on the club scene still and hadn't achieved the fame we know of today, they were small potatoes, Nine Inch Nails' little brother. We decided to pursue a show with them; we begged the guy who booked Club Babyhead to let us play: please, please please, he said it was a bad match but laughed at us and begrudgingly said okay. We showed up in three or four cars, no van, our trunks open with drums sticking out, to see two blocks worth of people standing in line around the corner. We thought positively, "This show is huge!" We shuffled past these pissed-off teenagers in long leather dusters, they looked like Columbine types. Inside there was a floor-to-ceiling wall of merchandise, all sorts of "road crew" schlepping things to and fro. We were awestruck at the 20+ different t-shirts, this was a merch mecca. Thirty dollars a pop! The club itself was dark, black walls, typical sour beer and bathroom cleanser smells. It seemed like a block of sweaty cheese just dripping from the wall of all the parties and shows and goth night events that probably took place there. The stage was about three feet high, broken wood, duct tape all over it. Marilyn Manson had already sound-checked; I mean, what the fuck, it is only 3 pm right now. We set up and left our gear on stage, we "back-lined" it up against the second band's shit: Monster Voodoo Machine from Canada on tour with Marilyn Manson headlining. They had braided goatees and shit, real jamokes. The door opened and the merch table flooded like a feeding frenzy. It hit me right then, seeing these fans, that we were quite fucked.

For some para-suicidal reason we decided to be confrontational. John Von Ryan was the only person who smoked up that night and he went out first, yelling at these people that, "We are the police!" We had on our powder blue leisure suits. We looked like their parents. When they realized we were not props who Marilyn sent to mind-fuck and molest them, that we were honestly going to play music, we were going to double down, shit went off. We played one song and people spat at us; some fuck threw a quarter right at my Les Paul guitar and took a chip out of it. I went ape and started kicking kids, some fucker in a baby doll dress with what appeared to be hockey pucks pierced into his earlobes unplugged both sides of my pedal and tried taking it. I reached down and grabbed it. I looked up, Eric was backlit. All of a sudden everything got extremely slow. There was steam in the air from the hot lights above the stage. I saw this "tribal tat" guy try to pull Eric in the crowd, they really wanted to hurt him; all I saw was Eric step back and kick this dude's head back, heel to the chin, total whiplash. I saw this projectile; I thought it was a bicuspid, but as it came into focus it was definitely an incisor. A concert goer's front tooth had erupted from his mouth and flew through the air lost forever on the floor in the gumbo of cigarette butts and Marilyn Manson fans' bodily fluids. They all backed up. We might have played one more song or we just broke down fast and ran off, I honestly can't remember. Either way I was scared.

Time significantly sped up all of a sudden. We rushed backstage amongst yelling and loud jeers. Our two or three friends, the owner, and John Von's brother J. Ryan were backstage with us. Some knuckle-dragger yelled, "hit him with the pipe," and this guy came at Eric with a piece of microphone stand. Eric ran out of the club like a ninny with Jen and Craig and they left the rest of us there. Out of the darkness some guy came up to us yelling some illiterate shit real loud; with every other word he emitted this whistle sound from his mouth, he'd say something like, "You (whistle) guys (whistle) fucked up my (whistle) frondee." And we kept saying, "What? What does this guy want? Frondee, fondue? What do you want us to do? We don't have any food in our rider to give you, I'm sorry. Do you want some gum?" We thought he was talking friendly, about equipment borrowing or some shit; perhaps he had a disability. We quickly realized he was informing us rather coherently about how we had kicked out his front teeth and how he was from Canada and U.S. oral surgeons won't take his dental insurance and we ruined his tour because he'd have to go home to Canada... Look, you want anarchy in the U.K., well here was anarchy in the U.S.A., what do you want me to do, go carve you some George Washington tooth-shit? He kept steam-boating on about it, whistling away about some shit like Thomas the Train. We left. Marilyn Manson hung out of his tour bus door, he had on a wife-beater and no makeup, he looked like Steve Perry from Journey, he said, "Who was that band? I heard they were nuts," then went back into his domicile. We'd always try to debrief and process these things when we saw each other next; it was another show.

Around this time we actually felt good about ourselves and we made the tape with John Maclean – *A Demo Tape*. He was cordial with us and I think that Six Finger Satellite had set up a basic beginning of their studio in Pawtucket, RI. This tape was recorded at a friend of Maclean's, the guy from Small Factory who was a nice chap. We did about 3 takes of the 4 songs on that demo, some are on our posthumous release *The Stolen Singles* retrospective CD. The tape was the best thing that ever happened to us up until this point in our history. We designed the insert and the cover which was a photo of this odd oil painting that we used to take to every show as a prop and hang up behind us; it was some bad art we found in a dumpster, a guy's head with a goofy grin, but it went with everything else. We always had stage names and in the beginning mine was Manual Labor, and Eric's was William Tell. Eric, Steve, and I wore 1970s leisure suits; there were so many at Salvation Army stores, it was very out, so we'd find these really beautiful ones, nice ties, buckled shoes. Andrea had on a waitress style dress, perhaps a vintage Dunkin Donuts uniform. We'd sweat away the nights together, dripping these songs out.

On one of our excursions up in Massachusetts to go to some huge flea-market we had seen a Moog on some guy's blanket; ironically while we drove home to get more money to buy it (I was 10 dollars short, I even offered the guy my sneakers, nope) Ben McOsker had also gone up there, saw it and bought it for the $70 the guy was asking, balls. Eric and I had driven by, on the way up there and back, an archery shop, something in some guy's house of course, but out near his mailbox he had a huge bow and arrow made out of steel, perhaps a suspension from some massive truck or something was the bow, the rest was welded together. We decided to steal it, we had my little red Chevy S-10 pickup, so why not? We drove by a bunch of times casing the joint. We pulled up in front of it and decided to uproot the thing, throw it in the back, tie it down to the roof real fast and drive off. We hopped out and tipped it and holy fuck, this thing had at its base a whole axel from a truck tire and all that held it up, it must have weighed 500 lbs.; ire-friggin-gardless, we summoned super-human-ape strength and hoisted it into the back of the truck. It was prone to righting itself and standing up straight, which was almost 15 feet in the air, initially we barrel-assed away down the highway with it sticking straight up. We pulled over and fucked up our backs tying this monstrosity down. We did make it back to the space with it; after much hacksawing and chipping at rusty shit we got the bow and arrow off. We painted it silver and there were a few shows where Eric stood middle stage with that thing, it was theatrical, it was awesome.

Going out and being good friends was what we were all about, this was a lifestyle for us. Back in the day when we'd go out for beers, Steve was very much on top of whatever was leftover from the 1980s, Metal, Danzig, that Bono je ne sais quoi, but this was the 1990s. Steve was a ladies man with Journey-esque long hair, picking up random 80's rocker chicks back in the day all the time, perhaps it was out of his system? In the future, throughout the duration of this entire band, Steve never chased women, except for a few fringe harpies that pursued him really hard. Steve was respectable and kept out of trouble on all levels, he avoided conflict; he was a good guy. He was probably the best looking guy in the band, but something prevented him from being as horny as the rest of us.

Sitting in my Israeli occupied apartment I recall Eric and I discussing the finer points of William S. Burroughs for hours and hours; we talked about El Hombre Invisible's "cut up" technique. Eric was working on cool words to toss up in the air and he left for the night, back to his place not far away. Whether he used the technique or not he presented up with Arab On Radar. Right away I was excited about this band name. It said something edgy and at the time it was subversive, perhaps far more so now, but we were thinking about music and how we wanted to be perceived. We closed the Umbrella for the last time. The first real show we played on our own was at Club 3's in Newport, RI on Halloween. Our first gig with Craig as our drummer, we took my parent's minivan down to the seashore to our first gig as this new configuration of Arab On Radar.

Time passed and our confidence grew a bit, got a little stronger, we felt good! Andrea knew Marcellus Hall, the singer of Railroad Jerk, through John Maclean's Six Finger Satellite connections. She got us our first show *on the road* with Railroad Jerk, playing Sarah Lawrence, an all-women's college. The bassist was a junkie; we met him in the stairwell crying about missing his children. There was some micro-aggressive controversy about our band name, these students wanted to interrogate us prior to granting permission for us to perform our art. These identity politics were not all-consuming in the musical scene these days so the whole process was a prototype of what was to come and it all was a fool's errand because we were just retards who hadn't the slightest clue or capability to be politically correct about anything. We were just polite and said we wanted to play, they gawked at each other and our idiocy made us safe, I guess, they guessed... The show was in this downstairs bar, real Animal House vibe. They were looking for Otis Day and the Knights; we were not Otis Day and the Knights. These mimbo aliens didn't give a shit whatsoever, they were guests from a neighboring male college who were administratively allowed access to this "social," these frat guys, Ken dolls, with sweaters draped over their shoulders laughed and partied with reckless abandon. Poontang was the only thing on their mind, that and whatever jungle-juice shit they mixed up in the garbage can on the way in, it was grain alcohol and Kool Aid with an unidentified powder (probably roofies) mixed in, no joke.

Somehow another clique of people consumed me; it was the students from earlier. I went back to the women's dorm, a woman asked me in a Marilyn Monroe voice, *"Do you like Cognac?"* She proceeded to get me really drunk on expensive cognac, which I had never tried or heard of, and she dragged me to her room to have really wild and vile sex. Red head. I was basically molested at an all women's college, but I guess it can be seen another way. Green-lusting-carrying weight... throbbing for it, the band, the music, I'm not sure I'd ever been so excited in my life for what was to come. The future seemed bright. I had a pregnant radiance; my hair was shinier.

Chapter 7 - Animal Traps

We met Jeff Toste of the band The Laurels. The Laurels (later Bossman) consisted of Jeff, Dare on drums, and Ryan on guitar. Jeff was slightly older than us and we always considered him an authority, it really seemed like he knew the Music business, and of course we did not. There were basic pet peeves we had about their band, Ryan strummed his Travis Bean guitar like Dave Van Ronk folk or something. I can forgive him for that because he went on to develop lotsofnoise.com which was the go-to website for all things musical in Providence throughout the best years of the scene; it is an amazing archive. At this time, with The Laurels, there were existential issues also, things that bothered them as much as us; Jeff routinely jumped off of Dare's bass drum, ovaling it, which really pissed Dare off. One of our first tours was with The Laurels. This is where we really learned the ropes, learned our schtick, learned that it took more than the average song and dance to do anything meaningful in Music. Alas, again, or perhaps to teach us a lesson, our van broke down on the side of the road and we had to get in their van, all huddled up like the Roma, travelling to the next unknown destination, counting our gold. At one point on the tour with them, very late at night, on a long drive Jeff drove and I rode shotgun. I woke up, slowly, looked around scanning the perimeter of the environment I was in, I looked back to heads laid back sleeping, snoring and saliva dripping, everyone out. I looked left and Jeff's head was back staring at the roof, mouth agape, snoring too. There were many turns, so G_d must have been on our side and maybe he was driving for a while, someone from the back screamed, I was in a complete freeze response, like watching a movie, then the van turned, screeching the tires, fishtailing but planing off. I give Toste credit for handling it calmly, he was an ace, but there was a period of time, perhaps 20 seconds, 40 seconds, 2 minutes, more, where we were barrel-assing down the highway ghost-riding. Jeff was so fucking determined all the time. We angrily convinced him to just pull over, pull the fuck over, anywhere, so we stopped at a rest stop, the kind with just benches and a restroom/outhouse type of deal. We were so crammed, carsick, and insane, I remember taking my sleeping bag, exiting the van in the warm night, and just sleeping under a circular metal table in between the round seated metal chairs bolted to the concrete. I slept under there for two hours; we were in Texas, there were massive webs under there and a 4-inch spider, under that table. I thought, "Fuck it *is* true."

Hours went by, looking up confused, yet more drama was about to unfold. I woke up to flashing lights in the parking lot behind the van. Jeff very quickly got into an argument with the cop. He just began right away saying, "Officer, why are you harassing me? Please stop harassing me or I will have to ask for your badge number and request the supervising officer to be present…" It got bad, but thankfully the cop left; I think the cop just didn't want to do the paperwork. Later that morning Dare told me that during the police encounter he had woken up just in time to throw his t-shirt over the four-foot orange bong they had. It was so suspicious. These crazy fuckers would travel with this mega-bong seated right between the driver and the passenger seat. You'd look in the windshield and see the driver's head, then this orange tube in the middle up to the roof, then another head, the passenger, as they were pulling in anywhere. Exasperated, we left and ended up staying with Mat Brinkman's brother in Texas. It was a rescue call and he was cool enough to shelter us from death.

Around then they lost Ryan and gained a new guitarist named Eric, they changed the band name to Bossman; this configuration of musicians, really amazing, great songs and show, but often they seemed pissed off at the world, some injustice somewhere, some micro-issue shit in Chechnya. They had all these Noam Chomsky books and were always discussing heavy shit. I chalk it up to high empathy levels and total cortisol-induced road-stress.

Onward, Jeff would convince us to "jump on bills" rather than actually book shows. This became our business model at the time. Often the hottest bands, Blonde Redhead, June of '44, people who had nothing in common with us, be it musically, class-wise, or personally, were tragically stuck with having us open for them. The funniest of all was The Make Up. Against their will, they had to tolerate us. They had some corporate tours lined up that we managed to jump on three nights in a row: Cleveland, Toledo, somewhere in Indiana. Awkward shit like that. They spent so much energy and labor avoiding talking to us, you'd think they'd just get on with it if only for the sake of not having to work so hard not to: Capitalist's dilemma. There were booking agents, definitely in Cleveland, that got off on manufacturing these little messy, silly bills. Perhaps it was a passive-aggressive response to whatever corporate shit storm they had to weather, booking The Make Up, you know, "riders," all sorts of pomp and circumstance for this idiotic James Brown white-guy bullshit. The Make Up always waited over an hour in between our set and theirs, regardless of what fucked hour it was, 3 am? But the mod squad would wait for it. How else would they get laid, until whatever time the Godfather of Soul Ian Svenonius came on. It was embarrassing all around. Who played who? They portrayed themselves as uber-PC, but we had no response to that. All the gospel rip-offs, how far can you go throwing stones in glass houses? Ian tried to talk to us once, something like, "Cool set, I like your stuff." We were just raw energy and too far gone to respond in any rational way, the chicken flock had its pecking order established by now. We heavily lusted after Michelle (bass) and everyone knew it. We were all about their use of audience participation, but she did not like us at all. We played with them at Speak in Tongues, we were obnoxious and aggressive, the stage was 3 feet up and during The Make Up's sound-check we feigned setting up our merch, any excuse to be on the floor, we all took a peep as Michelle set up her gear in a miniskirt, from our outpost vantage point we saw heaven. Eric Paul had a bloody nose from earlier and it gushed before we went onstage, some allergic thing, he came out and said "you have good coke in this town." It was a real Dirty Dancing scenario, and we were the bad boys. We laughed at such bands and I'm sure they laughed at our poverty-stricken punk; we were peasants to them, lower animals. One thing they had on us was that they were driving to stay at a paid-for hotel and more often than not we would be homeless.

The dude at Speak In Tongues had good taste and a big heart, he agreed to lock us in the club overnight and come back early in the morning to let us out. I recall the urinals in the basement bathroom being rival to CBGB's in their filth and stench, but he used them and so did we, sometimes at the same time. That night just after he padlocked us in, the local bar must have let out and we were sleeping on the stage, with mice crawling around, which turned out to be a lesser problem. Some drunken gangbangers from the bar started thrashing on the metal door, trying to break in, yelling that they wanted last call. It got real scary for while.

We were up at about 8 AM and he let us out around 11 apologizing for oversleeping. We said our goodbyes. We had nowhere to go so we decided to go swimming in Lake Erie. We walked down the dirt, which I guess you could consider a beach, and ironically the dude was there with his girlfriend too. We all sat down and had a nice day. The lifeguard kept calling us out of water every 15 minutes due to radiation. This place was like a melting reactor; you probably would end up glowing in the dark if you stayed in too long. I vividly recall a little kid who looked like Fat Albert pooping in the water, I told Steve who was out farther than I as we swam frantically for shore; he screamed bloody murder as we both verified seeing *the log*. We had already ended up drinking a lot of the water. I guess this is what immune systems are for.

Over the hills in faraway lands, we used to play such places as Ann Arbor, Michigan at The Blind Pig, to no one. Although, one true stomping ground where a few people did like us was the town called Ypsilanti. We had our local mate, John, who owned/ran a café there. John was in really great physical shape, mentally positive, he had a Zen outlook on life. John sat behind the counter at the café, making us all some of the best juice concoctions I have ever had in my life, "hints of pear" I remember him saying, these were gourmet shakes. He also, of course, had a crush/relationship with Andrea. The café in Ypsilanti was where I met Iris, a passionate local sculptor who had her work on display at this venue, it was the month of her gallery opening in the front of the place, we just happened to be playing there then. We really hit it off, I needed her so bad, we vibed on romantic talk and light petting. Very late at night after the show I remember her spontaneously wanting to sculpt, she was always producing art and was not tired at this particular moment, Iris was inspired. I left after the cafe with her to her studio where at her request I disrobed the top part of my body and sat in a chair talking for hours on Philosophy, Literature, Art, Travel, Love, Lust, Filth and Cuisine. We stayed up until the sun came up all the while she was sculpting this bust of my head. At a certain point, we were fucking at her studio, we regained our composure, then she gave me a necktie as a parting gift, bad luck for men, was this on purpose? So much of real romance is not like the movies; it is more like sculpting it out. That bust allegedly stayed on the wall at the café for many years after. We never returned to this home away from home, but people would tell me it was there, that it got moved to a glass case now, then who knows? Maybe destroyed...

We would play for very few people, but those times were good, sunshine for shady people, bright happy times. It was always a safe haven for us. John would always try to get us on the best shows. It really must have sucked to have been an established band like

"The Make Up" or "Blonde Redhead," because of course in NYC, Chicago, Philly, DC, the entire West Coast, they wouldn't even acknowledge our existence and would scoff at us. No booking agency would ever consider us or let us open for anyone of substance there. But, dear readers, all touring bands have to *get* to these big towns, and therefore must play the Ypsilanti's, the Providence's, and that was where we had serious muscle. We were underground heroes in that our audience was organic, we stayed until everyone was gone, we played (irrationally) to no one so many times, we shook every hand, signed every record, played our hearts out to those who came to see us and people knew it. Not all of these shows were malicious, we played with the great Zeni Geva once in Michigan and it was mutual respect all around. But these elitist bands that existed during this time of musical history, the ones who obviously bought their way on to the scene, paid for it dearly by having us, their worst fear, "jump on the bill" in every in-between town. We had groomed these towns for years and we knew everyone, we were all down to earth comrades. There was nothing they could do. These were pirate tactics at their finest and we were fucking Greybeard.

Something else interesting, it was around this time of the band when we decided that we would be switching from leisure suits to Work Clothes, Dickies. I initially had some abstract idea about plumbers and how they look and exuding a neutral aesthetic. Ironically, I used to work as a plumber's apprentice, wearing the Dickies was no joke, doing "honey calls" was not fun. It was always symbolic of our working class status, but simultaneously it was a throwback to the Bauhaus movement of the 1920's, industrial influences, in this sense the uniforms were used as an artistic statement. Shutting down some of the senses in order to give the sound a more present role in our performances. The Dickies uniforms we wore were an effort to create a tabula rasa for the music, perhaps a bit of influence from the Heaven's Gate cult. They took on a life of their own. Our good pal Chris Spohn made us the unique belt buckles that completed our uniforms himself, four flying vaginas, each in different states of sexual arousal, what a great gift. I think mine was the most aroused, Craig's was dry. We started feeling confident and rarely wore them unless we were going to play. It was militaristic and became part of our ritual. We also were done with relying on the club's PA and lightings, most sound personnel could not, or would not, veer from the norm and mic up both of the speaker cabinets we used (big fucking deal, 2 additional microphones) and without that we sounded like The Bee Gees on a very bad acid trip, with the sound guy's failed attempts it was even worse, so we played very, very loud, situated most of the time on the floor of the venue. This occurred after years of frustration with the sound situation but ultimately worked out quite well for us. I came up with the idea to use 500-watt Halogen work lights which saturated us in white light, white heat, they cast great shadows, accentuated the monotone uniforms, the lights fed the treble panic attack aspect of the music. We were wicked hot.

The closest we came to a return to our old haunts in Michigan was years later when we played Michiganfest; somewhere out there in the World there is a DVD for sale of this event. It was freezing cold that night, snow… The place you would load in was some sort of long corridor, perhaps a freezer entrance at one time. I remember the band Deathcab for Cutie rolling in, very late. Perhaps mistaking us for servants or utility workers for their benefit somehow, they pushed their amps toward us. They said, as tough as they could muster, trying to sound all John Wayne, "Yeah, we're Deathcab" and we just started laughing as they walked by, jeering at them "… for Cutie!" They were frail beta males so nothing happened whatsoever.

We usually did not come out on top for pretty obvious reasons; we never meant to be so irritable, but having such a huge failure of understanding regarding our music over and over really grated on us. The rejections and slights drove us to play better and better, practice harder, play until physical injuries occurred, nerve damage, living the enlightened sounds. Sometimes we were our own worst enemy.

Chapter 8 - Termites Without Ties

Amongst other moments, we had a gig scheduled at Upstairs at Nick's in Philadelphia. We were booked to play there, well, just Bossman was. Jeff ran upstairs while the opening band was on; we were late. He asked if Arab On Radar could play, which seemed like no big deal, but they said No adamantly. We decided on Jeff's advice to blow this show off, he drove to another club, the name of which I cannot remember, to ask if both bands could play. We waited out in the van anxiously. Jeff came back happy and we got the green light. We loaded in, and did a basic sound check, our equipment was onstage. Those guys were headlining, since the place was so small they didn't load in. Hours went by and Jeff was taking all sorts of calls, talking to people in Philly, we were thinking such great things were going to happen. At about midnight, we started this conversation that somehow started like a chimney fire. We were thinking that maybe Nick's was the better gig. This escalated into a manic panic, and Jeff said Bossman was indeed going to try to go back over to play the initial Nick's gig, then come back to see how things were here. They were even considering double-dipping to play both shows (rather Capitalist). We were thinking, "Fuck, we are blowing some huge opportunity over there," the walls closed in, it seemed like everybody who was nobody but thought they were everything was at the other show. We somehow strong-armed Craig to go do the necessary skullduggery of telling the management that we had to go, I think he told them his grandmother died or something profoundly extreme like that. In an insane move we just broke our shit down, a few people came to see us, we passed them as if something real wrong had happened without making eye contact. We loaded out. Philly is small, this network is tight-knit, we should have known, the guy from that club called Nick's and gave them the heads up that we were coming back. We poked our heads in and immediately shit got hostile. We figured this out pretty quick, Jeff came running out and we all ran, time sped up and by 2 AM it was over, we panicked and we sped the fuck out of this city before we got our legs broken. Yet another night sleeping in the van at a rest stop on the highway, bathing with psychotic truckers, writing to no one on postcards that never got sent.

In addition to being in bands and touring, Jeff Toste ran his label Heparin Records, which put out *Queen Hygiene II* our first record. This was a very big deal for us and we were very grateful. He was trying to make something happen in a forest of darkness; the man was passionate, he taught us the hunger for success and set the standard he knew one must hold to make a dent, he was pushing the envelope further. Jeff taught us that at least you could say you did something, once it is out there it can never be erased.

The road teaches you that there are times when you are on the bottom and there are times when you are on top. You learn when to just put on the wig and duct tape the porno mag to your back, but other times you're the stud who has the pleasure of getting some; just something to consider if you are going on tour. There was one time, I believe, in St. Louis where we played a "jumper" show. We were commandeering a gig from the band June of '44. Of course their guarantee was about $350, regardless of the fact that most people were there for and appreciated us. This was classic for an up-and-coming band like ourselves. We drew the crowd, but we played too early, everyone left, they played to virtually no one but got all the money. Promoters sheepishly apologized and paid us nothing, turned out the lights and went home to watch *Frasier* re-runs. I vividly recall after that June of '44 show ending all of us in the band sulking in the parking lot, cold, hungry, and without gas. I guess I turned into a street urchin, I partially snapped mentally as I walked up in back of their van. They all wore gray V-neck sweaters. I knocked on their van, real loud, which must have startled the shit out of them because they could tell we were feral animals, disheveled with lice, like unfriendly beach-dogs. I said bluntly, shaking and really angry, "we have to get to the next town out of St. Louis, we have no gas money, give me $20 right fucking now." Whoever it was, my recollection the singer, in a moment of terror, just handed it over. We had no choice but to do this. This is why I never get angry with those from the barrios, they have no choice but to rob, it is nature. You should feel honored to be part of that evolutionary chain; it is tit for tat. When touring in a band during these times musicians had to accept that the rules of biology applied.

It was about this time we embarked on the mission of living life on the road. There were times riding across the countryside I felt such beauty. I carried myself like Levon Helm from The Band, I was important now. The landscapes and the billboards, we always joked about our travels. Leaving Providence we were amped. Equipment loaded, everyone had their stuff: toothbrushes, toothpaste, butt creams. We'd never feel as though we were "on tour" until we left RI and were into, typically, Connecticut en route to the New York area, the westward trail. We regulated our weed smoking, no pot until our sacred spot, North Stonington. We would always blaze there. The next milestone was Mianus: just about the time the THC hit our brains in the best way possible, that road sign would appear. Many stoned hysterical laughing fits occurred about the residents of Mianus (my anus). Ironically, Eric would always tell the tale of his high school girl friend from that town, we'd cringe and laugh at the implications, going to a movie in Mianus, eating in Mianus, fucking in Mianus, he just talked about how difficult the drive was to see her. That was when we were touring, that was when we were "on the road." We had gotten our groove and felt comfortable at out-of-town shows. In the mid-1990s not many people had toured like this, we were blazing trails. The road became our entire life, being out there somewhere in the unknown, we'd run away with the circus.

1 Retard   y
2 Barnyard   y
3 Herpes II   B
4 184   B
5 Swimming   B
6 Herpes I   B
7 Attack on Tiajuara B

This era was around the time people's fashion shifted. What we used to call "Romulans" became the rage. It was basically a look akin to Dr. Spock from Star Trek, bowl-cut hair that was genderless and pervasive. The Romulans were our fans.

On a wayward trip West we landed in Louisville KY, we'd usually play this barn-like place called the Do Drop Inn, many times; it was an intimate venue, I recall Jeff Mangum and Polvo and all those types dominating this folky scene at this joint. They came expecting something like that, but got us, our testosterone clashed with the Art kitsch on the walls. The place had rafters which I recall Eric and Steve both swinging off driving the owners into a panic about liability insurance rates I am sure. We met some really nice friends, a great guy named Jack, a 50-something-year-old gent, who flirted with Andrea, wanting to "give her a bath" and other gross shit. I recall him taking us up to a Southern mansion of sorts, showing us the fields of tobacco he said were owned and protected by the Kentucky Mafia (not the Providence good fellas that is for sure), in the middle were massive pot gardens surrounded by tobacco plants, that was their game. Jack was sort of like that vampire step-dad guy in Lost Boys, "Max," they could have been identical twins. Great vibes; parties galore were had in this house, in this town. All the sweater-rockers were there. The final time we played Louisville we went astray and played a local gothic/rock club named the Mercury Paw, things were different, none of our friends came out to that place. I recall playing until about 4 AM to hockey lovers, I went to the bathroom at the end of the night, urinal stalls side by side in a horseshoe shape around the tile floor. There was a steady cascade of vomit dripping off the walls and about a one-inch puddle of precipitation that I plodded through to find a stall in the far corner. Slosh, slosh, slosh.

Back East we played some hostile shit show in NYC. No one would put us up. We left dejected and drove on. For whatever-the-fuck reason someone, possibly me, thought it would be wise to trek out of NY across the George Washington Bridge, you know, Jersey, no commotion, nice cheap hotels, rest, fun relaxation! Jersey! The whole state stinks of chemicals, cigarettes, and some sort of strip club guido-spray cologne. Over the bridge we went. We got our second wind and drove a while, this too we thought was an advantage, get to the next gig faster! We ended up in Trenton or Rahway or Newark, some fucking where. We were now all beyond exhausted. Pulled into this random drive-through looking place, a motel. Typically, we all ducked down and once again Andrea played her part and went in, sure, single lady in a huge van, 3 am, just passing through. We were such bastards, I remember us pressuring her into carrying all our bags in herself which meant multiple trips from the motel to the van and vice versa. We just hid, like rats, pothead paranoid lab rats on the floor of the van with our beady eyes. The parking lot was bustling, like real traffic, so many people milling around. We peered out watching pimps, hookers, drug addicts, dealers, skinners, johns, tweekers, and other pieces of shit drunk loudmouths traipsing the lot. A woman with hot pants on, someone probably named Candy or Sugar, walked up to Andrea and accosted her. She/he thought Andrea was moving in on her space, her turf. She threatened her but also made a very empathetic offer, protection as it was, from Freddie the pimp. I mean, six trips to and from the van, then four dudes get out, then we all go into the motel? Hell, Sugar wanted in on this shit! She had somehow quickly changed into a cheetah skin bikini and she wanted to join in for a cut. The room itself was a marvel. All I can say is, "purple fucking rain." It was lavender with a mural of a nude Nubian goddess on the wall holding back two leashed tigers in some Franzetta-esque *Conan* comic. It had a heart-shaped whirlpool with a built-in stereo in the wall. Mirrors on the ceiling. Andrea had her clothes strewn all over the room almost like she had given herself over to the prostitution aspect of this all. We were all too tired to see the irony. But the real irony was we stayed there, fucking going on all around us in the surrounding rooms. We three nerds on the floor, Andrea in the bed, all she wanted was sleep. I recall the four of us schmucks getting up and going for breakfast; Andrea stayed in the room, sleeping until about noon, total payback, retribution. All was quiet there during the day, total silence, serene. That door with three deadbolts and some sort of electronic locking device the size of a phone book on the inside was all unnecessary during the day. Everyone was mopping up, mopping up the cum, the mistakes, the guilt. Everyone reassessed their worth; in this jungle we all knew where we were at in the food chain.

Around this time, once we got back home, we hunkered down to write some new material. Six Finger Satellite was always busy, recording their album *Severe Exposure*, I think, acting very pro. We had moved in to The Parlour, their studio to practice; we sublet a separate room that they usually were not using and they needed our rent. I had this huge garbage bag that I wanted to drop off at Goodwill full of old clothes, mostly my girlfriend's unwanted stuff. I had to make room in the car for our equipment so I took it in The Parlour. This was the first night I had my new Kramer guitar which Travis Bean had designed when he worked for Kramer before branching out on his own. We got too stoned as usual, hour upon hour of very loud endless jamming had ensued. Out of sheer boredom in between jams I went in the clothes bag and got out this very small knit grandma sweater. It was white with a purple doily collar, one button. I took off my shirt and just put this on, it was way too small for me, those guys laughed. We started up our racket again, mid jam the door just busted open on us. I remember J. Ryan just looking at me, rolling his eyebrows like Groucho Marx, questioning facially. We kept playing a bit and J. and Maclean were pointing at me laughing. It was embarrassing, when we stopped, although the guy had rarely said two words to me ever, Maclean came up and wanted to see my Kramer. He didn't make eye contact ever and spoke in this low, weak voice, but what a dick, him and J. laughed about how if his ever broke he'd call me and something about me being an imposter; at the time we were, in an innocent way. It should have been a compliment. In the later days of Fort Thunder when we were kings of the scene, they never crossed over from that early 90's Sub Pop club scene to the new dirty boulevard Art loft scene. I remember thinking, "How do you like that purple doily collar now bitch?"

It's amazing how, just playing regular music, the Led Zeppelin, AC/DC, Pearl Jam, you can excel at that type of music and make a really good band, and you're always in the parameters of what's "acceptable music." One of the most mind-boggling things for me was stepping outside of those parameters and operating out there. You can come up with something that's such an amazing idea, but if it's not accepted as the norm, and if you're seen as being outside of the parameters, it blows my mind how people can't hear that or even consider it. Which is why if you read our interviews and reviews over the years you can see that people were just repelled by a lot of the aspects of our music. It took us probably until after the band broke up for people to even begin to understand that what we were doing wasn't just cacophony. We wrote some really good music at this time. It was growing to be much less derivative and more unique, not sounding like much else that had already been done before by greater people. But once you hear all these amazing musicians that broke out of boring mainstream music, you can never really listen to The Ramones the same way again; we were breaking out ourselves.

Chapter 9 – Audio Transmission Fluid

In the early days, we were trying to write structured songs. The difference with *Queen Hygiene II* was that we were trying to be "straight players." When we performed *Rough Day at the Orifice* live, it was weird, we didn't necessarily have our own audience for this new music so it was a lot of heavy judgment by people, which was fine, they ultimately ruled in our favor, those that got it, the weirdos. For the rest, there was always Radiohead; lattes go down more smoothly with Radiohead.

I played a Kramer guitar, which was the prototype Travis Bean was working on, then he branched out to have his own business. I'd seen Steve Albini and John Maclean (buddies) play them and I wanted one so, so bad. At the time they could still be discovered. I was in Tennessee during the trip we did playing the early *Rough Day At The Orifice* songs. I walked into a dank pawnshop, and not even looking, I spotted one. The guy only had a few guitars in this shop, alongside rifles, lamps, various keyboards etc. I said, "how much," and he replied, "$600." I said I only had $300, he took it, ranting about how the thing couldn't stay in tune and how heavy and ugly it looked; he shamed this guitar. I didn't feel too bad about it, when I was in the parking lot I nearly pissed myself. I bought my other one, the Standard, in Providence from a Brown University student, probably because he needed quick money for blow, for $800. It was great to have these tools while writing, recording, and playing the "Rough Day" songs. I was listening to a lot more jazz, Albert Ayler, Sun Ra, Miles Davis *Bitches Brew*, other odd music like Fela Kuti; Eric and Craig hated it. They'd listen to The Strokes, who I fucking hated. I experimented with ragas in this new tuning AADDAA with the top A loosely tuned down to a low octave A. This is what I played from that day forth, listened to all Ali Akbar Kahn and Ravi Shankar. We liked *No New York* so much. It was around this time John Roman mentioned US Maple and Melt Banana. We heard of Skin Graft Records for the first time. All of this motivated us very much to do better; it raised the standard. We felt that as different as our music was, that as a much longer project, we fit in well with these bands. Some of the emphasis went on the drum beats and we all gave input into the off-time, tribal tom tom, blast beats in these songs. It is some of our weirdest material. We played brutal. We were wearing the Dickies plumber uniforms. In a cultish way I suggested we all shave our heads; this was met with adversity, Steve's hair was always long and Andrea was very particular about hers. But we actually did it. This really freaked people out on that tour. It was like Synanon had come to town to abduct them.

1 Retard
2 ~~[scribbled out]~~
3 HERPES I
4
5
6
7 Attack on Tiajuana

People ask a lot about recording *Queen Hygiene II* itself. We wanted to record with Steve Albini to be one of the bands in his stable. We never ended up even meeting Steve Albini at the time, I think he avoided us, but his cohort and master electrical engineer Bob Weston crushed on Andrea, she loved it when Bob displayed the vacuum arm on his high tech marble turntable; the way it gently came down, I have to admit it was so erotic. Things went well between them and then Bob was kind enough to fly all the way from Chicago out to Providence to record us. We had huge plans to record at a guy named JJ's brand new state-of-the-art studio called Sound Station Seven. At the 11th hour the session had to be moved, it was treated so formally as if Kurt Cobain himself (already dead) was going to attend. We ended up recording that entire album at a studio named Normandy, which has an interesting Rock history of it's own. New Kids On The Block, Tom Petty, probably hundreds more important people recorded there, the gold records adorned the wall as we walked in. This guy Phil Greene ran it; he let us in and we began. There was some mild problem at first because I think Bob wanted to recalibrate the tape machine and it was obvious to Phil Greene we weren't worth that hassle, so we didn't, we didn't care. We had no idea what we were doing. Bob asked us for our production ideas, jokingly saying, "You want to sound like ZZ Top's *Rio Grand Mud*, right?" We neither got the joke nor had any retort. He taped us using all sorts of microphones that were odd-shaped, three on each guitar cabinet, all sorts of shit. In the end we did a bunch of takes, did minimal mixing, and went home half-scared, half-excited. We had to pay a shitload of money to have it mastered properly. It was all good stuff. Jeff Toste passionately embraced it; we all thought we were doing something very important. We were so obsessed with our live show that it seemed to not matter too much. We got artists Mat Brinkman and Brian Chippendale to silkscreen an amazing album cover and a great insert. We picked them up still wet off of the racks at Fort Thunder and hopped back in our van to go back on the road.

Universally, during this clueless time, when we scheduled tours we didn't even book shows, we just loaded up our homemade wares, various tapes, t-shirts and posters and got in the van and drove. We went as far as Pittsburgh until we finally had to stop. Our approach was to see if we could get on a local radio station, play our demo tape, then somehow a person would hear it and agree to give us a show. Ill-advised method in hindsight but that is how it was. We did sell LPs from the back of our van on the street, we took to going to laundromats and begging for places to stay for the night from absolute strangers, we met many friends this way. Someone took pity on us and directed us to the local vintage clothing store where the owners were in a band, hoping they could help us with a show. Fortunately for us they did. We played to no one in a place called nowhere. The next night we played a Polish restaurant where we met - John Roman - he and a friend were eating pierogies and we had a solemn gig on our voyage West, we felt as if we were playing a chain restaurant, but in all actuality it was a local hangout. We had no expectations, we played to no one, but after the show he spoke to us with deep respect. We found a kindred spirit in this man. He was also a little standoffish in a xenophobic way, but we managed to win him over.

I seem to remember Roman, or a friend of Roman, living in the Squirrel Hill neighborhood; he was living in a frat-like situation. It may have been a nice chap named Doug Mossarac, I am forgetting, but I do know it was like hanging out with Peter Brady, swell. I recall him telling us to keep it chill because nights earlier people at this location had a wild party which resulted in the launching of a garbage can full of glass beer bottles off of the flat roof of their apartment down to the streets below. The residents who were pondering whether bagels from Kulikov were bigger than the bagels from Lemberg were not very happy about this act. This was a Hasidic neighborhood by and large; this act was not appreciated. Roman always had a sneer of guilt about him, a chuckling British sense of humor, such a funny guy. I remember sleeping at this other locale, a skid row apartment with Jeff Schreckengost and the other members of The 1985. There was a foul-smelling sewer, some sort of open sewer where all of the street vented into the apartment; for fresh air, you allowed entrance of a smell. The smell was namely the morgue next door. I slept with my face near the vent, imagining the washing of cadavers that went on nightly wafting in my nose, the smell of death. Of course, I was so happy to see Roman in the morning. We always had coffee together; this man was a mensch and he was in the band with us as far as I was concerned. I respected this brother's pain, his story, and his contributions to the musical cause. We kept coming back to Pittsburgh to play for years no matter what. It was like visiting family.

I felt like an extra in the movie *Deer Hunter* every time I was in Pittsburgh. Bridges and beer and Warhol and Rusted Root. John Roman lived here and we'd call it "Roman's Empire," lovingly. He had so much musical information, he knew what was going on in Chicago, maybe because of proximity, but the guy just had a loveable attitude and was a funny bastard. He'd keep us in the loop, bands, stories, tales of shows his band The 1985 played, often with great bands. On our days off here we would always go to the Warhol Museum, one particular time there was a Mapplethorpe exhibit, bullwhips up the ass and all that, then we got high in the bathroom and went to the third floor to play with the huge silver pillows, giggling. Pittsburgh was an essential stop for all bands then, we'd always go to these Carnegie Mellon parties, sometimes awkward ones, maybe even some gender studies book club gatherings where Chablis was served. It was fun, everyone was uncomfortable, but there was drinking and good times.

We kept grilling Roman about venues to play in Pittsburgh. We thought it might be better to play bigger, weirder joints and do our own show, but he was always like, "no, no, Manny would never allow it." He'd tell us of how Manny would call bands before shows and yell at them about playing other places other than his promotional shows; they'd resist and he'd offer them money to comply and all did. He had a lock on Pittsburgh shit! He owned Carnegie Mellon and muscled Mr. Roboto Project, he had everyone preferably play the venue he booked, Garfield Artworks, which had as legendary a presence as Manny did. It was so odd and funny because everyone in the band besides Andrea got triggered by Manny; she, alternately, would sit and chat with him for hours. I remember walking across the room towards them when she was talking to him and finally

87

getting close enough to hear her whispering in a motherly tone, "Tell me what you feel right now, what do you feel when you call Jeff a cock-blocking fucking asshole?" I mean, she was reprogramming this motherfucker, what a saint she was. He was a real bastard though, always giving us shit, playing too short or loo long or being too violent (not that he cared but we might break his microphone.) He was a psycho-schmuck, we used to bust his chops about wearing a hat all the time, he *never* took it off. Roman would tell us how he'd seen it off and how scary that was. It was all in good fun. Manny loved Andrea which leveraged us on to a lot of great shows; when she left the band we'd slowly feed him updates on how she was doing, but only if he was nice. I'm happy for him and she rehabilitated that wild motherfucker. Roman told us of a party he went to where a girl somehow talked Manny into entering a dog cage and how he let loose in some catharsis of BDSM shit. Good for that dude, kiss the boot of shiny, shiny leather, Manny! He was a real character, our label Skin Graft would send him a tube of promotional flyers, really, really nice silk-screened posters promoting our tour and we'd get to the show and see none hung up, then we'd talk to him at his podium and chair at the door of the venue and see in a huge pile of bands' tubes, our tube; then after we played he'd be sitting next to our merchandise selling those posters to people and keeping the money because they were his to promote the show. He'd compromise and give us a cut and be nice. It was always about keeping him sedated. He yielded all the power and was brilliant in his Machiavellian ways. It's just that, bands are already stressed enough, we didn't need a pimp, so we battled to keep him preoccupied, sent him looking for duct tape a lot. Then he'd go tell his enemies (because he was an army of one) to go buy some on their way to the show and he'd let them in for free, then deduct that cost from our pay as promotional expenses. This went around and around, but this was the only way we played great shows like the ones with Melt Banana and US Maple in Pittsburgh. He needed a dog cage so badly, it was like once he gave up power he was a great guy, but that rarely happened, and it never did for us in the later days. We cautiously played on...

We had throbbing erections all of the time, like Chihuahuas we'd just lay in our sleeping bags "pitching tents." These were rock hard, pulsating, sweaty erections; they were nobody's fault, so don't be afraid, they were pure chemical testosterone situations. Every once in a while a mysterious hand would come over the seat and stroke it a few times, these poles, never seriously, just in passing whilst talking, usually asking questions about Men and why we are so fucked up. She would have liaisons on the road too, we were all horny, she was an empowered woman and we were like adolescents. This probably was a sadistic feminist motivated act, but those few strokes sure felt great. It was a tad incestuous because she was a surrogate mother/big sister/aunt-like figure to us. We were always beneath her and she was the voice of reason. She did her own thing. She had been through it all and was so much more worldly than we were, that went unsaid. We never questioned when she'd want to be away from us, it was like a mom needing respite from her ADHD kids, we were hyper delinquents and she just needed a fucking break. We were the obnoxious little brothers.

Floors, floors and more floors, sleeping with my head in the cat bowl often. Playing to no one at Sudsy Mallones, a laundromat/club in Cincinnati, begging a random woman who was doing her laundry to stay, she let us, but had to get up for work in the morning, I slept with my head in the cat bowl on her kitchen floor, that cat was quite upset. Solid cat food like Meow Mix is very comfortable as a pillow, Friskies, not so much. The smell is what gets to you and the material itself, it sticks to your face leaving brown imprints all over, not good for your complexion. It gave me a rash.

So often we had hours of down time before gigs in these days, we weren't doing much else, and the rare short drives to the next town would allow us hours to investigate the town once we pulled in. We would shop for records and books. In Columbus, OH there was this bookshop that had a really amazing pile of pornographic magazines, it was a typical tchotchke shop with all sorts of cool shit in it, but we were interested in going way in the back where no one went. We would tear in there every time and pay $20 a pop to purchase these really raunchy European porn magazines. Of course these became commerce in the van, like prison inmates we'd trade pot for a "borrow" of someone's porn-stash for a power-wank. It all evened out in the end. Steve and I went to look at a music shop. There was this old 1970s PA system, one that was once owned (no word of a lie) by The Pure Prairie League, the band that sang "Amie." Steve and I talked the shop owner into letting us buy just the two Tweeter cabinets, I had a theory that they would sound like Steve Albini's gear, somehow. It didn't, but our adaptation, getting amp heads with two outputs, running one to our 4 X 12 speaker cabinets and the other through the Tweeters produced a tone I called "natural distortion" meaning we did not add any effects on the amp, just ran it clean but the Tweeters overdriven gave off a holy racket of a sound. This racket became our sound, treble. It seemed like Steve and I had finally arrived at a long, long sought after sound that we had searched every nook and cranny for over so many years. This was it and it was unique. I think I could stay with you Tweeters for a while, maybe longer if I do.

We were playing a house show in South Carolina, a real punk house, in a bad neighborhood. This place should have been condemned, a real building inspector's nightmare, bowing floors, rotted flooring, smelly, dog hair everywhere, you know. Punk domain. We arrived early and met up with our buddies in Bullroarer who are Collin and Tom who would later be USAISAMONSTER. We were skateboarding, hanging out in the afternoon. The show itself was uneventful, there was a habit at punk shows to overbook the bill, every one and anyone who wanted to play with Arab On Radar just did. So from 6 pm until 4 am it was just back-to-back bands who all sounded like Black Flag tribute bands. At night, after we played, the house was infested with people, so we all sat out on the front wall. It was about 3 feet tall, concrete dropping off to a sidewalk, then the street. All night drug activity was going on. How many times has that 1989 white Oldsmobile with tinted windows and 4 passengers circled the block? There probably were about 30 people sitting in a row down the wall, kibitzing and getting stoned, talking. There were no girls, pretty much just a sausage party. The Olds comes back and Dunk! A loud sound with a whimper to follow, a punk went off the wall backwards. Apparently the locals picked up a piece of asphalt and threw it out of the car, hitting this kid in the forehead, knocking him out. Some minor mayhem and empty threats ensued, hubbub about nothing. Around 3 am we decided to crash. The house was still moshing with 50 people inside, no respite there. It was so fucking hot there was no way I could sleep in the van. Collin went inside the house. I decided, for whatever reason, to sleep under the van. I guess it was just the coolest, safest place to go, I was feral at this point. Tom was frustrated and decided to camp out. It was dark out in the back yard.

It was probably about 10 or 11 am, I was probably the first person up. I went to the backyard and saw Tom. He looked odd, like he had leopard prints or something, as he came closer it looked as though he had gotten in a mud ball fight. As I looked down at the punk lawn I realized the reason no one went back there was that it was a landmine field of dog shit, all sizes, all solidities. Poor Tom slept well but rolled in a seemingly endless field of dog shit. In the dark night there was no escape so he just rolled with it... I'm not sure the shower worked here so I think they just ventured on to their next show, parting ways on our separate tours, we didn't hug goodbye. I found out years later one of the guys from White Mice lived at this house long before he moved to Providence. He moved to our city and built out Munchaus, an iconic loft space we all played at.

Florida was a wicked strange place. Very early on we played in the panhandle, crossing over to South Carolina. We played a meaningless show to ourselves and one guy, who looked like a very normal, neutral person. We went over to his house afterward; there were very few items in it. He had a fish tank that was empty, no water, no Angel Fish; this is always a bad sign. We started to get really paranoid when he said, "I don't sleep." He kept going in and out all night. We concocted a theory that we were being sized up for murder or to be cannibalized and that he just kept going to the hardware store for whatever he forgot, duct tape, plastic wrap, a shovel, roofies to drug us with? We got really scared. He was gone in the morning; we just locked his house and drove away at 5 am just to get the fuck out of there. All the other psycho shows we ever played in either Florida, Delaware, or Brussels, all had this same vibe.

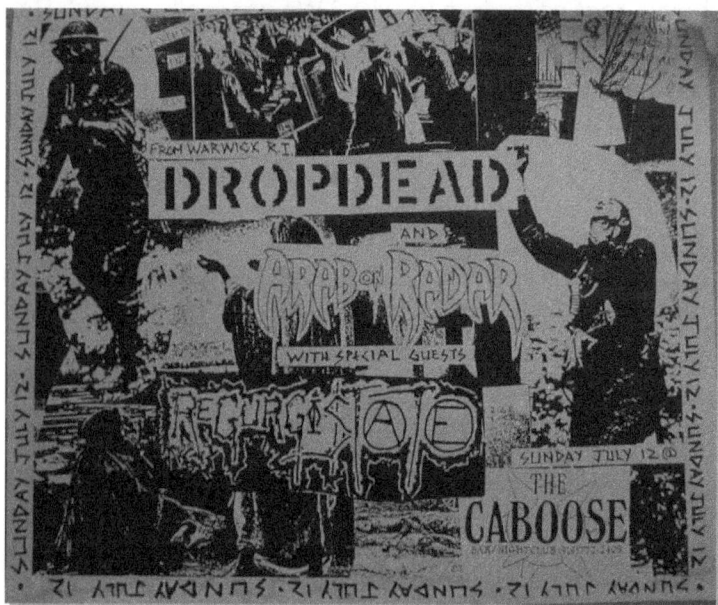

Andrea had known Ben Barnett and Bob Otis for while and seemingly out of the blue Dropdead asked us to do a part of their tour with them. It may have been at this time when we bought our van to go with them. This was a great opportunity for us, we were thinking of shows, with people, to play for! It had been five years of solitude. For Dropdead this was a bit tricky, we were not hardcore punk really, I mean, there was that one "blast beat" on *Queen Hygiene II*, the song "Attack on Tijuana," that was the song Bob and Ben mentioned liking. Perhaps that was enough? It wasn't. Regardless, we got the show itinerary which included legendary hardcore venues like ABC No Rio in Manhattan, NY., Stalag 13 in Philly. We were so psyched; it was like "Maximum Rock-n-Roll," which I'd read since I was fourteen, was going to be a reality, and it was, all of it and the unseen. We had our van, some flip flops, gear, a tote of shirts and records. Dropdead was a rolling fucking record store, their own P.A., massive amps, pro guitars/bass/drums, their own box of microphones, contacts, they were really geared up for battle, all black Antifa clothes, Ben dyed his hair blue and had a down Mohawk. They looked great, scary but fucking hardcore. This invitation was so much more than just shows, they invited us into their world. We would have never had the opportunity to meet or speak with the people within this subculture, anarchopunks, afro-punks, legends of hardcore. Honestly, most of the songs, to me, sounded the same, that homogeny has a turnoff to me personally because my angle on the whole thing was making new avant-garde music. This was more about the message than the song. We didn't have much of a message other than readings from traumatized raping sexist poetry which was not taken seriously by the crust punks. I remember one gutter punk calling Eric "Eminem!" due to the lyrics, which in hindsight, he does look similar, but I digress. We would never dream of speaking before our songs, what would we say? "Hello, I'm scared." If not for Dropdead endorsing us every show probably would have went the way of the Marilyn Manson one, but to the credit of the hardcore scene, Bob said "listen" and most did. In reality we did sound like Crass at times and if you look at old No Wave flyers there were shows Crass played with Sonic Youth and Teenage Jesus and The Jerks. No one cared or considered that, we were there because Dropdead vouched for us. There is little else more Providence than that. We were "dear friends."

Dropdead had a fully-extended van that towed this massive homemade DIY box trailer made of plywood which was chock full of records. They brought a silk-screen press with them and on day shows (we usually played two shows per day) Ben and Devon would press shirts right there at the venue; they worked so hard, these guys. We just smoked pot. We picked up our albums and t-shirts for the road from Mat Brinkman hours before we embarked, panicking at the 11th hour as usual.

The shows were great at some places, at others, not so much... For instance, ABC No Rio had a vetting process for bands who play there, and there were problems that some scholar had with our lyrics, and probably the bright colors of our first album... I mean, it wasn't black and gray, so...

I think Bob or Ben helped smooth it over with the bishops and we were allowed to have access to play. It was a bit frigid, because all we knew how to do was either fuck with frat boys or turn out the art school kids from RISD to Cal Arts, but we survived. House shows were better. We played two shows in Chicago, one was an all ages matinee with Los Crudos. This was amazing. Martin was a great singer, gay, Latino, teacher. This guy should be the President but I bet he wouldn't take the job, but wow, what an inspiring human being. The hardcore argument won me over because never in the artsy scene had community and hope felt so real. This was 1998, remember. The upsides were plenty but one fact of the hardcore scene is that they support you with "the Love" and definitely not the money. Our pay, deep in the bowels of some squat somebody cracked, typically, consisted of a huge lukewarm kettle filled with overcooked pasta and runny red sauce, you knew they had too little sauce and just added water or some liquid. I just wanted to go the fuck back to Providence and eat some real Italian food.

Tragedy (no pun intended) struck in small town named St. Cloud, Minnesota. Now, mind you, the way Dropdead booked tours was that there was such a tight-knit hardcore network, they would just post on their website and say where they were going to tour to, people from all over would write them and offer all sorts of shows. It was so very opposite of our approach of begging booking agent shysters and cold-calling people who would rather be snorting coke off of their partner's ass-cheek. St. Cloud was a gig booked by someone with a dial-up connection. We rolled in like the Pope's convoy into this one-horse town, passed some row houses and slaughter shacks right out of Upton Sinclair's *The Jungle*. We got to this boarded up building, looked like at one time it was a grange or mason's hall, some shit. It was drizzling out. I remember Ben kind of prying open a piece of plywood covering a door and coming back saying, "there's nobody in there, dude." He has a low voice, most sentences from Ben end in a low "dude." Anyway, we called the kid, this was early cell phone days, flip phone pieces of shit, we called and called. He told us, "Bro, I contacted you. The show was cancelled." Many threats and shaming "not cools" were slung at this prepubescent virgin show promoter. He knew he was fucked because he would now be shunned and his gestures toward atonement were ignored. We left the "venue," or not, what the fuck, our fuckin' van wouldn't start. It had been running weird for a few hours prior to reaching St. Cloud, but now it had *dropped dead*. Some of us drove around in those guys' van to find someone in one direction, others walked to see if anyone was around to ask where a mechanic was. It dawned on me that the whole time we had been here we had not seen a single human. Very few cars, no one. It was silent. I went with the foot crew, me, Eric, Craig, Steve, Bob Otis, Brian the Dropdead drummer. We must have looked like the Mongols had come to town, just walking around looking so weird. We saw what seemed to be a slightly hip thrift store. We walked in to an open shop, no one in there. From the back of the store out from behind some rug-like curtain door came a wiry guy. He had long hair, almost looked liked Jesus but on heroin, a post-Crucifixion Jesus lets say... He wasn't a junkie surprisingly, but he was shocked at the sight of us. "Who are you?" "You're here to play?" We said Arab On Radar and he started talking about G_d and Mohammed, sort of discouraging Muslim beliefs but talking highly about the Christian life. He wouldn't let us go. Bob said they were in another band.

"Oh yeah?" he replied.

"Dropdead," Bob said.

This guy lit up like a menorah, his face gleamed. "Drop Dead? Oh my word, this is a sign."

He invited us back behind the curtain where there was a big open room with a stage, a real piece of shit drum set on it, metal folding chairs, it had an Alcoholics Anonymous vibe. He told us this was his church. These kids were around, mostly African American, little kids, 5, 9, 13, 17, they all came out of who the hell knows where. These were his kids, he said, a big family church. He told them G_d had sent Drop Dead there today; a miracle had happened. He gave us some beers, like Corona Light or something he had been keeping for the carpenters working in his church. We indulged. The guy brought out all these comics he drew of Herculean Christ fighting demons. It was his fantasy work he drew. Some of the comics had him fighting and decapitating drug dealers; it was uber-Christ fighting the wrongs of the Earthly world. They were great. As time went by we figured we should go, he kept begging for us not to leave. His eyes were locked in on Bob, blood shot and almost worshipping him, sweating, begging Drop Dead to play. We kind of pried his arm off of Bob and left fast. Later on we realized that there is a wicked popular Christian band Drop Dead, which in this case almost made sense. But we weren't it. At about 8 pm, in the dark rain, it seemed like 40 days and 40 nights, finally our van was fixed. We drove by the arch in St. Louis at about 5 am. It was raining real hard now and we saw it, small, from miles away. Perhaps it was G_d's way of keeping us motivated.

It was around this time in our musical career that I saw the first signs of feminist rock with this band named The Need. I am sure many others had preceded this band, Bikini Kill etc., but this was the first band we played in the same touring circuit with that was pushing identity politics so hard. It put identity above music and I suppose I used to be much more upset about this back then, but to us this was a great offense also. We had always played with females and besides a few slights we did not see a huge sexist situation around us, perhaps we were just tone deaf, but I think not. I remember an all female band in Providence and this real douche-bag promoter (male) always giving them the hi-hat, but that happened to us so many times it was hardly attributable to gender or so I thought at the time. I white-knighted the situation and took him aside and demanded this band play after the crap from Boston band he tried bumping them for. It seemed at the time the right thing to do as a musician. It was like the Lenny Bruce days, we were all the "Act," and the enemy, quite often was the Promoter, us musicians had to stick together because we all were getting used and abused nightly. I've heard many stories from bigger cities of really offensive sexism and horrors of rape and harassment. In Providence, I do think the scene was always supportive; we had all the issues with the Black Hand, they ran everything and we had to cope with that. Plus, who the hell am I to tell anyone how to live, as if any of us know or are any better. I don't know, but I do know The Need sucked musically and the fact that people came out in droves to get what amounted to a support group on a good day and a lecture on morality on a bad one was just insanity to us. Someone, and I cannot reveal who, drew a Hitler moustache on the Hitler looking woman in that band's flyer picture. Their posters actually got hung up prior to their show (a minor miracle) and they were prominent at the clubs we were playing because they were booked on the same route only a day or two behind us. We all laughed at the poster, because it was a bit fascist what they did, thought-policing was their modus operandi. They got mad. They had promoters call ahead to our shows and they lobbied that we not play, all sorts of shit like that, "outing us" as bad people (which we were) and all these tactics which are commonplace today. It was the exodus of music for music's sake only, judgment by the ears not the eyes, and divisive. The dogma was enforced as time went on. This was not like hardcore scenes where homage was paid to all musicians prior, this was post-modernist thought, and the scene was a Skinner Box where all the gender studies homework could be demonstrated in action. We found it vile to reduce this creative, innate talent and hard work to politics, we were apolitical, our politics was Music. It was offensive that this attack on our scene happened, forcing this opinion on people as if it were universally true, bollocks. It ended up harming more than it helped in my opinion, but then again, honestly, look at where that opinion originated from and what we were like at the time. We never saw this coming and it deflated many of our dreams of a new music taking shape, where our contribution would be a revolution and all sorts of music like ours would take over and be reborn and resurrected time and again. Ironically, the American revolution attempt of the mid-1960s played out on a macro level very much like this, cannibalism took hold, identity was always there, but it was organic and aimed at toppling the system which came very very close to happening. Identity being atomized and fragmented, destroyed the momentum, pitted brother against sister, races against each other, power battles that made Foucault grin his Igor grin salivating in his triumphs, it became too big to fail, regardless that the argument was bunk and destroyed publically unequivocally. Religion rears its irrational head again and those who resist it are stomped, those who embrace it are healthy and happy, but their music still sucked, this is all I knew. Don't use Music instrumentally.

Amidst all this fanatical thinking, I got really obsessed with the situation that happened in Waco, Texas, with David Koresh and the Branch Davidians. I was oblivious to this being some right wing militia, whackadoo cause. I was intrigued by the fact that people lived this way, so different from my Judeo-New Englandy-prep school-artfag existence. It was on TV for hours, the first live-stream event to my recollection. Of course I hated the government with a passion but it was the first time I remember the media playing the masses in such a sports-like way: Will he give up? Will there be a happy end? It all turned into a horrid Todd Solondz movie where it ended with bar-b-que'd children all at the hands of a lying state/local police state. Genocide. It turned my stomach how they infused toxic flammable gases on those people, human beings, for what? Nagasaki, Hiroshima, these acts by power terrified me. What did these people do? Stockpiled rifles to sell, which in Texas is as much a venue of commerce as oil is. The religious fanaticism and cult aspect were mere side issues. There are government pigs who still live amongst us who decided to light a match to those innocent babies and children. It haunts my nightmares to this day.

So, we decided on our day off, a year after the holocaust, to drive to Waco. We didn't know why but I must assume full responsibility for passionately forcing the band to go. We grossly underestimated just how (I know, cliché) big Texas is. In our cobalt blue van with neon green paisley curtains we rolled in. Townsfolk helped us find the desolate farm roads, untraveled roads which led out, way out, to the area. There was a tree, not much else, an established parking lot. We saw some blown out school buses that looked like they were converted into living spaces or sheds. In the lot there was an Escalade with tinted windows, black on black. There was a tent set up. We approached the tent. This sunburnt homeless woman emerged, she had these elaborate placards, like a corporate presentation, on easels, perhaps four or five of them, with family genograms of all sorts, biblical quotes. Her name was Amo Rodin, an original resident of Mt. Carmel (the compound) not a follower of David Koresh, in fact, he expelled her from the congregation, but that is another book. Down here, we learned it was quite incestuous, and that long before the internationally-televised holocaust, there had been much history. Her husband was the original pastor and founder of the Branch Davidians, an offshoot of more spiritually radical sects of the Seventh Day Adventists, if you can believe that. A very tight-knit group, isolated and withdrawn from the community. Probably out of boredom, due to a lack of radicalization, or maybe due to being a musician, David Koresh challenged George Roden for his throne. A very Oedipal situation ensued and according to Amo Roden, this manic lady, David Koresh shot and killed her husband. He got off on "stand your ground" personal defense laws but she was bitter about this. Over time Koresh built up the church, drawing in all sorts of misfits from Ghana and Florida, some talented accountants, a potpourri of needy souls. As I mentioned, they traded goods "in town" and got into trouble with the ATF due to some unpaid license fee. The firearms were never even uncrated, they just had them warehoused and sold them at local gun shows, a commonplace activity in these parts. A pissing contest ensued and the rest is history. Janet Reno, the Attorney General under President Clinton, may you burn in hell.

Her sermon ended and the conversation digressed to small talk, we probed her about camping here and she warned us about coyotes and how cold it got at night. "Don't light a fire though, they'll come and eat us all alive." That was enough to convince us to sleep yet another night in the van.

We said G_d bless and all that shit and headed out to survey the scene. Everything had just been left after the holocaust, thousands of bullet casings, Nato rounds 5.56s obviously shot by the government strewn the area, burnt plastic. In typical government style they left standing David Koresh's Honda motorcycle that had more holes than Swiss cheese, some macho gesture that "they won." We saw all the buildings, the foundations where it all went down. I have a morbid curiosity for such things, like I have to be there, see it for myself or I don't fully understand or believe it. I have no doubt now my opinion is correct, once you see it you know. There was no reason for this. These people could have simply been waited out, picked up on arrest "in town" months later with no fanfare. It was similar to the plot of First

Blood where David Koresh played John J. Rambo. But ironically old Slick Willy needed something to distract from his problems. Never underestimate the power of a secret blow job, it might be worth burning children alive to cover that shit up. Fuck these people.

Back at the parking lot we were just hanging around morosely, nowhere to go, out in the lost. Somehow we split up, next thing I know Eric is talking to the people, the husband and wife, in that black SUV. They were some radical militia types, three-percenters, the fringe of the fringe, operating against all government, yet more folks who think they know so well how it should be in the world, they are that smart, you see... Not the type of folks that you'd just want to grab an ice cream with, you might pick the wrong flavor and they will blow you up with a homemade bomb. I see him get in the SUV with them, then very slowly they circle the lot. All we could hear is gravel crackling under the tires, real slow. I thought, "What in the *fuck* is he doing now?" He kind of flopped/jumped out of it, but they were not going fast, regardless he kicked up some stones and dirt exiting fast, and ran back to us at our van. He frantically told us how the guy was "off the grid" and how he had in the SUV all sorts of radios "untraceable by the feds, like in a moving cave." I think Eric still thinks about the black helicopters and other theories on how the world will end. I could clearly see how one could easily get brainwashed out here in No Man's Land. We drove out back to Waco proper, slept in the van at a truck stop, went on to our next show in New Orleans, long drive. We rode in silence. They were sick of my heavy ideas on life. It was only mentioned in jokes thus further. We'd say in a weepy voice, "They shot his bike, man, you just don't do that to a guy." But not much more than that. If the question is why, these things were a part of Arab On Radar. We started to really feel comfortable in the realm of insanity.

We had a fun time traveling and were fortunate enough to have time to stop at the Badlands. This place is so psychedelic. We climbed around doing all sorts of random jackass foolery. Against some of our cautions about National Park regulations Steve picked a beautiful flower. He hung it on the dashboard while he was driving. Eric couldn't drive because he had severe mental impairments or was a singer, so the rotation was Craig, Rob (our tour manager), Steve and I. It was always tense when Steve was at the wheel, lots of anxiety and stress radiated backwards into the van like a catalytic converter malfunctioning. He was responsible for that pollution. We looked at the cute prairie dogs for hours, then it was time to go. As we left, of course, there was this checkpoint, and also a big boisterous lady in uniform, a park ranger. I could tell by her hat positioning on her head that she was very "by the book." Right way she said to Steve, "Sir, why are you exiting the park with a specimen?" She went on a fucking botanical diatribe about plant life and how wrong it was to pick this one, then the conversation got low-brow because Steve apparently was dismissive with his facial reactions to what she was saying. She said, get out of the vehicle, which I wasn't really sure she had the legal standing to order, but he did, huffing and challenging her the whole way. She made him put it in a garbage bag and dispose of it in the trashcan; this was a lesson. The straw that broke the camel's back was when she said the plant was "noxious" and Steve just wigged out. "What did you call me?" he said, "what do you mean I am obnoxious?" She kept repeating, "No, noxious, noxious," and we chimed in half-pleading with him to just slow down the impulsivity and obtain a definition from one of us or the ranger. He plowed forward not listening or understanding. The funny thing about Steve was that he always does eventually get it, and he is a loveable guy so it is never really that big of a deal. We were all laughing afterwards, the ranger included, but man, it is hard watching those gears just burn up like that, there is no stopping that limbic system in there.

Way down San Antone, San Antonio, we drove all the fucking way down here. Of course it was the NCAA playoffs, we waded through so many people, driving at 5 miles an hour the whole way down to the Mexican border it seemed. We did see The Alamo, I thought about how funny it must have been to see Ozzy Osbourne piss on this thing, and I could certainly relate as drunk fucks walked past us slapping our window, heckling us in our van. We were scheduled to play at a pizza parlor with At the Drive In who I think booked this place or had some affiliation with it. Those cunts announced to the owner that they were boycotting us. We couldn't figure out if it was due to our name, or if they used this PC angle to cancel because they had something better to do which is the likely scenario. Regardless, we played to no one again, another pizza parlor gig, you know how that goes... I think we crossed the border to Juarez that night, did some deviant stuff, bought switchblade knives and came back, but I could be wrong, that might have been Tijuana some other time, too much fuckin' tequila.

jeff --- ██████████████ wrote: > jeff, > a couple of theses questions i had ideas about...but, let me > know what ones > you wanted to utilize ██████████ > and maybe we could discuss the others > i will also, re write those other answers > e > ----- Original Message -- --- > From: "lotsofnoise" <contact@lotsofnoise.com> > To: ██████████████ Sent: Saturday, February 16, 2002 2:51 AM > Subject: arab questions > > > > if you could go back and change 1 thing (regarding the > history of the > band), > > what would it be? That we ever tolerated this guy ██████ who writes for the Pheonix Newpaper for even one second. He should be removed like a rat in the basement of a family household. Just zilched... He has been the blind, blissfully ignorant voice of the current music press in R.I. for some time and he is incompetent. He writes week in week out sucking off ██████████ (his bud) and various other pandering pussies who kiss up to him. They supposedly keep him up to date on all things new in the Providence music scene. They fail. The problem with this is in every other town we play - Atlanta GA. for example, there is a good press liason (Creative Loafing etc.) where bands get an equal shake at thier artistic expression. ██████ that vermin) only knows lame old bar bands and boring rockabullshit that is so done so over it makes me embarassed to live here. Providence has had a great music scene for a long time and continues to... even though slugs like ██████ refuse to get a clue. He can eat my cheese, by this I mean ass-cheese. > > > > if you could have 1 new added talent, but had to give one > up, what would > > they be? > > > > what superhero would you want to be most? why? > > > > what does this mean to you..."Glory is fleeting, but > obscurity is forever. > > " - Napoleon Bonaparte (1769-1821)? when your short it sucks and you have to compensate by saying stupid little things like this... > > > > what is your take on human cloning and would you allow > yourself to be > cloned > > if it were free? No, because humans can not be cloned in the sense that we would enjoy... there will never be another us, only a twin-like lookalike (even that is debatable) of us and that person would probably be bothering us all the time and dancing with our women. > > > > do you think that someday we will find out that all plants > are > > thinking/feeling and the vegetarians will freak out? No, 99% of them will just start eating meat and project thier death anxiety upon another fruitless (no pun intended) endevours such as Yoga or raising "power children". A plants frontal cortex is quite like that of a vegetarians. Anyhow, the other 1% will live in a cave and eat stones and start bands called Inorganic Object. > > beatles sgt. pepper or beach boys smiley smile? Wings - "Wild Life" > > > > Buffy the vampire slayer or Slayer? They are no Joni Mitchell either of them. > > > > how have other providence bands influenced arab on > radar...both in its > youth > > and now? Yes, To say Dungbeetle inflenced us would be a crime to Dungbeetle, but in a very internal way the spiritual power they possessed shit... is something we will never forget... they made us want to do this stuff we do now. Six Finger Sattelite again, the same, they were so amazing at one time. We think very few people can imagine what it was like to see them really play... it was awe inspiring. Von Ryans Express plays an integral part in the spreading of our roots, they guided us to reach for that magic spot, that magic feeling. DROPDEAD was and is a band we respect so much... We remember back when our hormones were raging and we was all pimply and sweaty and they brought the house down in a real way, ya know, like last week or so... Just kidding about the vegetarianism stuff earlier, but the hormone rage this is for real. Now, we are not influenced overtly anymore by much Providence music, musically, but if you see us at your show then you are influencing Arab On Radar if we passed, then you are incapable.

Right about this time, Mike Hibarger put out our album *Rough Day at The Orifice* on his Op Pop Pop label. The art design was a bunghole of sorts, Mat Brinkman made the silk-screened covers and had cut his own hair (from which body part, I'll leave in the unknown category) and glued/sprinkled shards of it on to the cover. Some still exist from this original pressing, they are out there somewhere, his DNA and our music, what a deal.

We limped out playing shows, trying to make it to Chicago, we went through Gary, Indiana, Michael Jackson's birthplace. We always remarked on the industrial landscape going through there, chimneys of some sort that had flames shooting out of them. Gieger-esque pipes crawling up the side of a plant. Passing through Gary, Indiana, we passed the time trading Michael Jackson jokes, it just looked like hellfire burning, Hell, fucking Mordor. Pulling into Chicago, there was always a sweet cookie smell, it was always pleasant to be there. Once we hit Chicago traffic, we always felt better, there must have been a cookie factory near the highway and that sweet scent of Momma Chicago made us feel so good. We had scheduled to stay in Chicago for a week to record *Rough Day at the Orifice* with Weasel. He had a connection to a studio; we recorded there. I thought it was great, a minimal system that would produce the sound we wanted. We loaded in and managed to get levels the same day. Weasel worked hours on this and some aspects of the sound we were really on to it. We gave him our (much debated) elevator speech about what we wanted to do. Things have a life of their own. We left for the night and returned in the morning. It became apparent that some sort of situation happened in the studio overnight. My best guess would be that another "producer" who also worked there went out and got pretty lit up. The producer then enticed some people to return from the bar to his studio, a place presumably that would be vacant, a venue for late night cocaine use and further drinking, some unsavory scenario. The Bud Light bottles were removed from the mixing console and we moved on. The original mix had been edged towards extinction, a few tracks remained unscathed but the rest were probably moved by the ass of someone the producer was fornicating with the night before. He fucked on our album. Mid-morning we had our coffee and plodded forward. We got it back, we jammed the songs out, it was hot as hell. I look back at the footage we filmed of this recording in amazement. I was a twig, weighing so little, these were the moments that pure fanaticism takes over. We *had* to make this record.

While we recorded *Rough Day at the Orifice* at the studio with Weasel, we had to stay with Jeff Day, a local dude. We met many of Chicago's best musicians and artists. Jeff Day was a freelance journalist with *Lumpen Times* and their annual issue *Easy Listener*. We loved *Easy Listener*, we got every issue; there was one with Jeff Day really partying and Azita from The Scissor Girls in the buff. These were sacred tomes of masturbatory triumphs. We fell in love with this scene more than words can describe. In the times we performed, Chicago was the mecca of all weird music that we worshipped. Most of our early shows we built around the Chicago dates, these were highlights. The *Lumpen* mag was very helpful to the more underground bands, Bobby Conn, Weasel Walter, Jeff Day, and labels such as Drag City, Thrill Jockey, Skin Graft, and others.

The record stores nearby (the North Ave apt) where we were squatting were The Quaker Goes Deaf, Earwax Cafe, and Reckless Records. I believe The Dusty Groove was around then too. These were the places that we loved more than life itself. Jeff Day used to throw pretty crazy parties in that North Ave apt. We slept on floors, masterfully, we had these foam mats we used for comfort and in an area of this domain we rolled out our sleeping bags on them. By day we were out recording, and also by day Jeff Day's Rottweiler (who maintained the same party hours everyone else there did) decided to crash for the AM on our comfy sleeping bags, not before a thorough dog wash of licking every body part draped on my soaking wet pillow. The North Ave spot was nuts. Al Johnson of US Maple said, "Jeff Day is the only person I know who can turn a garden apartment into Amsterdam." This was the scene, we played at the apartment on the first day of our stay for the recording. It was fun, we met all the party people of Chicago.

Often we found ourselves playing naked often on the *Rough Day* tour. Andrea included. It was part daring ourselves to get crazier than the rest, and half sheer boredom. I remember a few shows in some basement, where a few people got the show of their lives, music, stripping, sweating and sex. Lucky for them. We were playing some of our best music, for some reason that album was overlooked, perhaps because we got much bigger by the next one and took on a new identity, perhaps the music was just too challenging for people. I associate it with Captain Beefheart's *Lick My Decals Off, Baby* album, stepped over, not *Trout Mask*, but interesting in it's own right, if anyone took the time to listen to it independently of all else. But alas, it came and went, the title *Rough Day at the Orifice* is fitting for what it was.

I never played extremely high or drunk, perhaps a beer or usually nothing at all. Total sobriety is how I went out working. I do recall one time smoking some chronic locoweed, I think we were in Bowling Green, Ohio. I got really, schizophrenically, baked. We went out, announcing, "We are Arab On Radar!" I jumped in the air and everyone but me made a sound. Train wreck, stop, embarrassment, shame, blame, they all looked at me pissed off. I was just giggling in some paranoid state. Of course, hup to it, problem-solve. I noticed that on the back of my amp, I had plugged my speaker wire *out* of the amp output and back into the other output rather than into the speaker cabinet. To add insult to injury, after I got it figured out we played one song but all of the music, rightfully so, sounded like sheer cacophony to me, nothing made sense. I was so lit that the sound was just something akin to a hairdryer blasting in my face and a bag of silverware being thrown against an oil drum repeatedly with my head inside it. The next song I couldn't even play, I just knelt down covering my ears screaming, "No, no, this sounds fucked up!" We bashed through it, but after I was lectured on "highness" and many a discussion about breaking up, calling it quits, ensued, this was common, we were always on the brink of separation. It was just episodes like this that made it apparent to all of us. Total derailment.

I don't know if you have ever done a backwards somersault, but if you have, capture that feeling in your mind. When we were embroiled in these meditative hour-long jams, that euphoric feeling took over. Spiraling backwards over and over, faster then slower, attaching to thoughts of the past, forgetting the moment. Sometimes the ideas would click, others, not. I'd conjure some feeling, like that very first time at the county fair where a Doors cover band played "Peace Frog," not the music or the notes, just that awestruck feeling I had as a kid responding to the power, feeling the people's reactions and body movement. This all came back as if revisiting a past life. Then my hands played some powerful riffs and it was only in this spiritual state of consciousness that AOR songs were written. Rituals had to happen, we were devoted. You have to ask yourself though, was it like this for our so-called peers? Is this how The Locust wrote songs? I am not so sure it was. We were priests in a way, with the baggage that comes with that role in the society of music.

I guess it was something that was pretty obvious but I was again quite clueless, looking at the facts, Andrea matured out of what we were doing. She was gaining a lot more other meaningful activities in her life than just hanging out day and night with us juveniles. She really took a liking to snow boarding and to her credit, she really got healthy and in great shape. I think we had some meeting where she told us she was leaving. It really broke my heart. It was like my older sister was leaving home or something, leaving us behind. But honestly there wasn't a second where we doubted what we were doing, if anything, the self-delusion and commitment to this cause just got more intense. She moved out of state shortly after that, and I don't think we've spoken ever since, which is something I really regret because I never had the chance to thank her for everything. Such is the Life.

We went completely fucking insane and wrote

Soak the Saddle in a frenzied fit of insecurity. There was about a day or two where we thought we should get another bass player, but I think we all agreed, and were so much of a cult, that at this point we decided to just proceed without one, which shifted our musical sound and performance in a totally different direction. Totally accidentally we fit in with what was going on, especially in Providence at this time. Odd configurations of bands, like drum and bass only. This was a good change for everyone. I mean, shit, what the fuck, what the fuck do you want me to do?

Over many months and the second we got enough songs to play, we debuted the entire *Soak the Saddle* album at Harvard University in a lecture hall. It was probably the same hall that Alan Dershowitz took calls from OJ Simpson in, then proceeded to teach law, it was a crimson carpeted room with people sitting way up in fold down seats. They didn't know what the hell we were doing on any level and I'm not sure at this point we did either. How could these people take themselves seriously academically, my brain triggered associations with long pulls off of cigars, back room deals, murder and war crimes, but everyone was there as if nothing had ever happened and we were some new thing to see. I try to not take that shit personally, but coming from where I come from it is difficult. Regardless, we were on to something good, something scholarly, and I guess you could say we were in the Ivy League of misunderstanding of the noise rock underground.

Every fucking time we played up in Boston there was a particular vibe; it's a business city and at the time there were very few fun things to do. That changed over time, but back then, this gasoline station attendant jacket thing was in. People would have a nametag like "Bud." Who knows how this caught on? Random clowns would accost us after we played in these geographical areas particularly. They had no qualms about stating their opinion about how we should get a bass player, how our sound could get better, how to make more money, how to succeed. If you think about it, what do people want? There is *the* best, if you want *the best* there are The Beatles, they were the best band ever, there will never be better. More money, time, innate talent, benefits of a particularly perfect time period went into The Beatles than will ever possibly occur again so just accept that shit. What we were doing was intentionally the way it was. We loved our own music for it was and we were highly insulted by idiotic comparisons or suggestions for improvement. Whatever you think about it we created and we weren't some fucking assholes that never came up with anything. Slight differences in frontal cortexes make all the difference, some are here, some are way the fuck over there. Either way, I hope you realize that it is *you* we made this shit for, otherwise we would have just stayed in our basements jacking off; we came out in a hope that you would like it.

Generously we had done a 7" with Load Records which was a really great thing, our first wax. Ben McOsker was a mensch at the time, a guy who had Providence's interest in mind always, a very selfless chap, I really admire the guy for that. Mat Brinkman worked on the artwork for this release. We had gone pretty deep into discussions with Ben about releasing our next album (*Soak The Saddle*). I had the idea to directly pursue whoever recorded the Lake of Dracula album, which was the most important album in the world to us at the time. Chicago was the mecca and US Maple were amazing, but when the Lake of Dracula album came out on Skin Graft we thought it was the best thing ever and it was. We scoured the record for clues and to our surprise it was Sonic Youth step-member Jim O'Rourke who recorded it. I always associated him, in a juvenile way, with PJ O'Rourke, no commonality that I know of other than name. Surprisingly Jim replied to our desperate e-mails saying that he had very little to do with the album, and the credit really lied with one Weasel Walter. We explained this all in another fan-boy email and Weasel agreed to talk with us. At the same time, we had to back out of further commitment with Load. Honestly, if I had had my way, we would have just stayed loyal to Load, but the pressure internally within the band led us to a very awkward sit down at Ben's apartment. We started off talking about positive stuff, about working with him, then Craig dropped the nuclear bomb and did most of the talking about how we, in fact, would not be, and how Skin Graft was the label we preferred. Ben got, understandably, very upset and we started to vacate before being kicked out. Bam! Craig simultaneously got irrationally huffy and stood up to leave, flinging open the door to the apartment violently, but it was actually Ben's utility closet. Lots of mops and vacuum parts sprawled across the floor as Craig submerged himself into the mess. We reversed out embarrassed and that was the end for a while. Silence... Gawking and eyebrow furled evil looks at shows was all we got from Load for a while. Ben confronted me, in the pitch dark, which was a misunderstanding, at a show and I responded very defensively and embarrassed. He didn't understand who pulled the strings on this one. He was foaming at the mouth, there was spittle at the corners of his mouth frothing like a latte. I felt bad because I admired the guy very much and still do. Load Records' catalog consists of the most interesting music, an archive that many have yet to explore. It will someday be unearthed and I pray it is by cooler people than we were to that guy. But time went on and the deal was renegotiated.

Like a band of gypsies, we were back out on the road again. It was in Atlanta, Georgia where we met these strangers. These people we grew to love as brothers and sisters were Pineal Ventana. We met them as if we both knew the secrets, that sometime somewhere we had transmitted important messages to each other in Morse code, as spies in the Moscow night. Once we got on some sort of circuit things traveled fast. It was an honorable affair. We stayed with a true friend, Kim Chee. She was such an inspiration in these times, she was so empathetic to us, she knew the scrambled eggs in our skull shells. We would do fun things, hit after hit, and she would always outlast us. I remember thinking "holy fuck" as we went along laughing and talking all through the night. We always stayed with Kim Chee. It was sad really, because I did love Kim, but like a sister, I felt really guilty at the time because I was shacking up with a totally different type of person at the time who lived in Atlanta. The guys would stay with Kim while I went off doing my porno thing. I recall sneaking into the van at 5 AM, breaking into it, because no one woke up at Kim's place until about 11 AM and I was hopelessly locked outside. Those fucks in the band would make fun of me and her, "their hips would lock" if they fucked, all this juvenile shit. Kim was really cool, we would always love talking and hanging out with her. She took lessons on sitar from guy in The Black Crowes. She always was cool. Pineal Ventana was her band along side with this great guy Jason who went on to own and operate a really high profile recording studio called Seizures Palace after he moved to NYC. I am so glad the guy finally made his dreams come true; he eventually recorded The Swans which I assume was a real thrill. Their music was real tribal shit, Annette, singer, kind of a wild-child. Partying galore. Fun times.

Sometimes psychosis takes over, worn and deprived. We were all in some traumatic state. What can you really say to people like us who were like that? We tried, talked about music... the singer was a free spirit, something kept her in check, but someone you felt was destined to sing. Everyone, cool, cool, cool. Great people. We always felt safe with Kim and all these great people, another home in the homeland.

I don't know where the fuck I was, perhaps it really was Atlanta, GA? Holy shit. We were late, very late, one of those many stressful drives where the shows were booked outside of the range where it was ever humanly possible to make it, booked by people who never actually drove it. By people who couldn't understand the risk, internally, of what it meant to put people like us under so much stress. The pressure cooker. We showed up in the dark. It was an *Apocalypse Now* environment, up the Mekong River. Bright lights in darkness. Kudos to them for keeping spirits high and keeping it going on. We were loading in, a long while after The Locust had played, after everyone had played, but still within the threshold where people, heads, were willing to stick around to see us. On the lawn leading up to the venue there were circles of people and in the midst of all the fog and mayhem, there was a big circle with much commotion. The story was Dave, the drummer from The Locust at the time, was some sort of MMA guy, a pink belt in Jiu Jitsu or some shit. He had frustratingly decided that while he/they were waiting for us to show, take on anyone and everyone who wanted to test his skills. He was out on the lawn grappling with a skinny hipster here and a fat guy there, a short guy, two guys, whatever. I walked out to see him submitting a skinny guy in a rear naked choke hold. I was so happy. I loved these guys from day one, before we ever met.

JP quickly said "hi" and that we ought to play, and out of sheer frustration/excitement we went on violent and technical as we could be. We played hard this night, it was a prison situation, or so we thought, hit hard or be somebody's bitch. We weren't anyone's bitch this night. In fact, we embraced the subtle loving kindness of raw strength and poetic warmth. We started an admirable friendship of mutual respect that night, East/West, kindred spirits without saying many words, we found some other weirdos trying as hard as we were and we knew it.

They all had that same hairdo, the one that was called unofficially the Romulan haircut. It was kind of a Herman's Hermits-esque effort to be cute for the fans? Girls? Kids? Who knows?

Anyway, I think that quite possibly it was Georgia where we first laid eyes on the guys from The Locust. We may have been there. We had coordinated by email and I attribute this introduction to the shows we did with Dropdead. Those shows both humbled and amazed me.

The fact that we did them was a true testimony to friendship and comradery. But The Locust was another thing. Let me try to explain it again, we walked up, very very late. We got lost, in a place much like fucking *Apocalypse Now* it seemed, the lawn went up and bright lights hit on us. Someone greeted us, an overzealous Locust fan through and through. They had a cult following. This guy told us the drummer, Dave, was some black belt in something and was grappling with people out on the lawn. I probably had blue balls but my testosterone was so up to see this. I gritted my teeth. He was there rolling on the lawn arm-barring people. I mean, I'm not a Royce Gracie, but this was cool. Violence was something we felt might do the people good at this time. We went in and met JP. I think people clapped for us that night because he clapped for us that night.

There were so many distinguished people we met around this time while we were on the road. We sometimes played a cool joint called the Fuse Box in St. Louis, real nice people. We played there which we loved *or* we played at this weird restaurant that we called Chelo's, but it had another name, we ripped our shit up while families ate dinner a mere 3-4 feet away, uncompromising, we went off just as hard as the times we played in bars or clubs; total bullshit level. That must have really been a shock for some normal folks. We usually played with a band called Pellum 123. Lucky for us they were super cool people who went on to be great friends with us, Pat and Heather Crump. Pellum 123 had some Swans influence, but they were closer to Crash Worship in the stage show, which was always bombastic. The first night we met these folks we played with Pellum and returned to the Crump's house, Pat had painted himself head to toe in white banshee garb, he ran directly into the shower to wash off. I had to piss wicked bad, he just left the door open to the bathroom and we chatted while he was in the shower. We laughed so hard once we both came out, because Heather said, "Did you know Pat has 2 assholes?" And I said, "No, I did not!" He proceeded to tell the story of how he was drumming and went ape-shit standing up while simultaneously knocking the seat off of his drum stool, leaving just the stand, basically a metal post upon which he impaled himself. It was quite serious, but they sewed him up at the hospital. He proudly showed us both buttholes, which to an unlearned eye, you'd never have known the difference between the two. What a gift, 2 assholes, imagine the possibilities! These guys were elegant though, polite classy people with great aura. We drank fine bourbon, some reserve from 1960. It was like eating caramel. Great times and yet another home, a sacred sanctuary where we could rest our heads over the years. The road provides such places and G_d, you are so happy to make it to them. I can't express how grateful I am to all the people who helped us over the years regardless of how many assholes there were.

Whatever, a year or so later we were on the West Coast touring and again played with The Locust. We finished the show and went back to JP's house. Immediately we sensed something was odd. We put our shit down near a couch and JP was like, "they are all in the bedroom, you can go watch if you like." So Craig went in first, then came out to get us. I walked in the back bedroom to see a couple, the woman on top with a clown mask on having sex with a strap-on with a young Latino lad who had a completely shaved body. The receiver was moaning like an oboe.   It was interesting, there were all sorts of Spocks sitting around the bed watching, guys and gals, I left after a few minutes, I think Craig went all in for the duration. He was like, "Scotty, tonight, don't beam me up." It was a great introduction to San Diego, if only I wasn't so depressed at the time, I probably would have went in to jerk off also, but I ended up just writing some letters to people who would never read them and then going to sleep. I cried a lot in these days.

There was one time we stopped at a restaurant before the show in San Diego, some chain restaurant. We all sat at this long bar at the place. It was us and The Locust and boy were we tired. The Locust had this van and towed a Uhaul trailer with all their shit in it behind. JP was always distracted, always calling someone or doing something that seemed, at least to him, to be seriously important and urgent. Consequently, he went outside to take a call from Elvis or the President or something. All of a sudden we looked out and saw some trashy motherfucker slamming him up against his Uhaul trailer. Perhaps he had started talking shit, the guy called him a fag or something and they got into it, but he collapsed right way, the dude wrote a check his ass just couldn't cash. For a strange minute he looked like one of those paddleball toys kids used to play with, boing, boing, boing. When it sunk in what was happening, I saw red. Steve stayed at the bar, the rest of us went out and unleashed holy fucking hell on this guy who was assaulting one of us. We beat this skank motherfucker down hardcore. Towards the last few minutes of this piece of shit's beat down I felt a hand on my shoulder, "Enough! Enough!" It was JP intervening. He was calling us off this bloody mess of a guy. I saw this as completely irrational, I mean this guy wanted to kill you a few minutes ago, where do you come from. Of course, when we let up he ran off and some bitch-ass friend of his picked him up in a car, he yelled some shit out at us about coming back with a gun. I was thinking, you stupid fuck, finish what you started. These people out here are not like people back home, you would never sleep with both eyes closed after something like that back in our town, you'd know that someday, somehow, that motherfucker who had not learned a lesson would try you again, perhaps when you least expected it, perhaps he would kill you, some rats have nothing left to lose. It was a learning moment for most of us. I guess it is better to live on the West Coast. I went in and ordered a grapefruit infused spritzer, I was thirsty after all that mayhem.

Touring south with Landed; we drove down, down, down, though Louisiana. We reached New Orleans and the wonders of the French Quarter. We played a show to some trippy people in The Big Easy. We ended up staying with Mr. Quintron in New Orleans at his Spellcaster Lodge. I tried to sleep on some fucking bunk bed but it was too hot. The lady from the club kept me up talking to her. She had a black Honda and we couldn't sleep so we stayed up walking around out near the stoop in New Orleans. She told me about her car that was out there, run off in a ditch, the Honda, she also said she had court at 8 am. We laid down for about 2 hours. It was about 102 degrees at night, sweating on top bunk of some fucking bunk bed, in this vampire's study, down in the mold, we bathed in each other's sweat. MC Tracheotomy was there, someone had on

"3rd Stone from the Sun" by Jimi Hendrix, it was nice, their pad had an uber-nice bathtub up on a platform, MC Tracheotomy was just sitting at a laptop. The sounds of the Jimi Hendrix song were a real cool vibe, heat was now 104 fucking degrees, not sleeping whatsoever, it was impossible, I kept thinking about my compatriot having court in the morning. Alas, Alex Chilton was nowhere to be found.

Our reputation was poor at this time, we were seen as GG Allin or Anal Cunt, which we weren't, but people got scared. There are so many scared musicians out there. We paid the price. We played to no one again and again, even here in this sacred place. They would rather see us sleep in their amazing place than play our shit, it was too out there even for New Orleans, go figure.

On our way back to some form of civilization, there was this old hobo, ironically named Willy that I was talking to at one of those roadside truck stops. We were both waiting, quarters in hand to take a shower. He told me a story about his life in the 1930s working under FDR's New Deal program the CCCA as a logger making camping sites and trails in the forest, perhaps in Michigan or Colorado. Willy worked with a crew and dealt with many personality types, from self-centered narcissists to lazy bums and everything in between. He kept longing for the end of the project when he can sit back and admire his work and drink one of the ice cold beers they had been hauling around in the ice box cooler. He finished, thinking the trees were so vast, an endless forest, everyday another meaningless tree, who cares what type or how dangerous it was to fell? No one is up here to notice. He smoked his pipe, a bowl full of delight. All they wanted was a trail and a campsite eventually. He finished up finally, only to find all the beer skunked, representing his depression and futile attitude toward the whole project. Years later, many years go by, he sees that the forest was not eternal and now seems small, dead, and that his work was all a mistake. He feels used and torn about his name being on the CCCA plaque as the original crewman who made the project, the campsites are now used by horrid people who pollute. The photographers and designers who went to rich schools co-opted the project, even though they contributed nothing more than some posters and other promotions of the crews work to sell it to these new campers. There was no moral to his story.

We headed our asses over to Houston, TX. We played this club Notsuoh, we pulled up to see the owner sweeping the sidewalk. Initially, I think he was bummed to be having this show. The guy's name was Jim. This place was amazing. By day, the first floor, a sort of community center where people played chess and read books. A functional café was run, lattes, fresh juice, a Class A operation. A really sweet lady who wore a Girl Scout uniform worked up in there. It had a little stage where perhaps bad poetry was read or some acoustic act could possibly play. We immediately started to brainstorm and complain about how the fuck we would play that stage. While the sun was up everyone was really supportive ensuring us it would be a good show. We had a juice and sat around for hours. Jim talked to us a bit at the bar. Time went on and he asked us to load in. We had some good laughs. We brought our shit in and he was like, "No not there, not that stage." We moved away from the beatnik podium and he motioned to go further down in back of the club where he opened this attic stairwell, a ladder basically. We approached hesitantly, but climbed up there to take a look. Once above we saw a massive open room, one frozen in time. The upstairs was a very old speakeasy that must have been a converted department store at one time. Up on the shelves were boxes upon boxes of vintage shoes, probably from the 40's or so. Dusty lamps decorated the shelf highest near the facade of the room. We realized this was something special. People smiled knowingly as we loaded our gear through the hole and up to this amazing venue. We blasted our shit that night, had a hot sweaty work-out-rigmarole. Afterwards Jim came up to us with a shit-eating grin on his craw, "Man you guys were great!" He wanted to party and on this occasion we all agreed. He told us how his mother was part of the old famous outlaw scene in Houston and how speakeasies were a part of living in these parts. He had a real rough side about the Law. It was some real heavy shit. The place was as hip as New York, he rented the other half at high rent (this is what sustained Notsouh I believe) to these Saudi or Egyptian guys who were really rich and had a very upscale bar next door. Everything was white in there. It was pretty obvious he had come over and drank on tap too many times without paying or something. These guys had a tolerant, "Hey, Jim," when he moseyed in. They were more than happy when he told them he was taking us upstairs to his office. We followed. Upstairs was a very elegant office, but dusty and untouched like a time capsule like where we played. He showed us his small card desk that he unfolded and this is where he did all the booking and managing the place. It looked near to impossible to keep the accounting straight for both businesses from a location like this but who am I to judge? Jim showed us this humongous wall which was all steel, it had many drawers and placards on it. He unlocked this whole wall to reveal a massive safe built into the wall, it was like something out of a bank. So cool, it was an outlaw's honky-tonk situation. We ended up smoking a bowl with Jim in the room with the wall-high old safe, we all were very drunk and when it was his turn to toke he started laughing at something one of us said, and he blew into the bowl sending sparks and all contents flying into the air at us. I was like, "Man, suck on that thing, don't blow in it. Christ!" He blew weed all over the room, a la Woody Allen in Annie Hall, but Jim was a total Southerner, he just laughed, hooted and partied all night. What a great time.

        We ended up in Austin, TX, playing with Black Rebel Motorcycle Club and all these other assholes, the show was for SXSW at Emo's with The Locust. Mike Patton and the bassist of Tool were there, we all got excited again about making it famous and living with maids washing our clothes and chefs cooking our meals whilst sipping mimosas by the diving boards of our in-ground pools... After the show we moseyed down to the main club let out area, a fight broke out on the avenue, some drunk hoodlums were duking it out, then along came a clatter and I looked back to see what was the matter. A perfect formation of Texas Rangers rode down the street just plowing people over with their steeds. A female Ranger perfectly executed a well-trained swipe and picked up the main instigator of the fight carrying him on the side of her mare down to where there was less of a mob formed. She cuffed his ass like roping a steer. This shit was professional. I remember looking at Mike Patton, we both were in awe, and saying, "Man, only in Texas."

Austin, Texas was a great town, we would play there a lot, King Coffey from Butthole Surfers came out to see us once, no one else came except him and one or two other people, the venue was big, he was sitting in the grandstands top row, no one else up there at this reggae bar we played. We were too green, he left without saying anything to us, we probably were amateur in a bad way, no respectable musician at the time would lower themselves to our level, no underground label would touch us. It was in Austin that we met John Syverson who went on to be in the band Daughters. And then there was the guy with huge balls, very large testicles which he liked to show people. His girlfriend Steph had this photo album of pictures she got from working at CVS photo desk, she compiled 100s of highly perverted, sick photos people had developed, a dirty dildo licking one, unicorn fucking, all sorts of shit and everything in between. On a glistening sunny day we went to a river, a big river, I remember going on a canoe ride with those 2 girls, odd ducks they were, they had a bond, they were the women who wore men's tighty whitey underwear with crotch cut out upside down as shirts, we saw beautiful giant turtles, I recall jumping off of pylons under the bridge, splashing in youth and making out. Later that night, us cowboys, we went to this really cool bar, I will never remember the name, but great drinks, real Southern, a dive bar, there was a framed picture of Richard Nixon on the wall. It was the best. Then we skedaddled out of town, two toots and a tat to go pardner!

Later on this tour it was no different, we were fanatical about records always, about gear, about clothes. We were always shopping like a bunch of Rodeo Drive wives out on the town during the day spending money, except we were usually broke. We were in Ohio, perhaps Columbus, I remember the marquis saying "Wu Tang Clan," why the hell didn't we go to this show? This was back in the Ol' Dirty Bastard days!

I recall this shop, a bookstore, the kind with just piles of books, books up to the ceiling, I think Craig discovered it, he was a porn detective. We went there on three tours. On a magazine rack they had all of these European XXX magazines. We would buy as many as we could afford. Of course they were $25, $40 for the connoisseur stuff, they were titled "ERO," the real raunchy stuff. I had never seen a... well, nevermind. We would masturbate without impunity at this time, always wanked without reservation, in hotels, in sleeping bags, in the van openly. We kept porn, our stash, as sacred as our pot, and we all kept score who owed who what on what level.

We were driving up from the South, at 4 pm or so, on a Thursday, up into the area around Gainesville, Georgia. We had time on our side. We decided to stop before driving all the way to South Carolina. We wanted the cheapest rate at the motel, so we ducked down and pulled into the lot. Steve was driving, he had on this Bret Michaels style cowboy hat.

Earlier in the ride into Georgia, it was hot as a motherfucker. It was my shift to drive, and the guys were going through their luggage looking for clean clothes. Steve had nothing but his jeans that were clean, so he decided, while sitting down, to cut them off, and convert them into shorts. We were exhausted. We rolled up in the blue van with neon green paisley curtains, into the carport of the motel. Steve threw on his black Chuck Taylors from our uniforms, and his V- neck white t-shirt that we bought a pack of at Walmart days before. We watched him out of the rear windows. He had cut his shorts off way too high. In the front, the pockets drooped lower than the legs of his cutoffs, the back exposed his buttocks in Daisy Duke shorts. He went into the office, oblivious.

We snuck in; we wanted to drink, smoke pot, and jerk off. We got our shit in the room. I had bought a bag of ice and a 6-pack of Corona beers. I filled the motel room sink with ice and put the beers in there to keep them cold. There was a rotation in order for whack-off time in the bathroom. Steve was up. He had already flipped his shit because his credit card was declined and he had to put the room on another one. He was getting pissed off at the person in India on the credit card customer service line. One hour passed, and we pleaded with Steve to let one of us cut the whack-off line, since he was taking so long on hold listening to Lionel Ritchie through the phone. He said fuck it, and let Craig go. All of a sudden there was a loud banging on the door. Steve motioned us into the bathroom. Eric, Craig, and I got into the tub and shut the curtain. We heard Steve talking to someone.

"Hey, you're here alone?"

"Yeah, just me, I'm on a road trip."

"Wow, all by yourself?"

Steve said yeah.

"You got all those beers in the there. Are you partying?"

Steve was so bordering on psychosis, he said, "yeah, my card just got declined and I needed to relax." The guy pushed on and on. We were paranoid, laughing hysterically but too terrified to come out of the bathroom. Steve escalated the situation, went outside near the van, and continued talking to him. He was the same guy who had checked him in to the motel. Steve always had this bad habit when he was under stress to stroke his hair and scratch his head. We went out into the room and snooped through the curtain. Steve had on his Daisy Dukes and was posturing like Marilyn Monroe, stroking his hair, standing on one leg. We heard the guy say, "Hey, be careful, they don't like this kind of stuff down here," and he motioned to our dashboard on which, ironically, someone had wantonly thrown the local music paper, it randomly draped open to the gay night club page. A huge pink triangle. Steve was very nervous. When he got back into the room he flipped out on us. "You assholes!" he said. We were like, "Man, go in, you'll calm down, it's all yours, thank you for doing all that." He went in. Then there was a pounding on the back door that interrupted Steve and his libido. Steve bugged out, he opened the back door, and put his head out, made promises to "talk later," all this... It was late now and we let him have his own bed. In our military lifestyle this was the highest honor.

In the morning there was this long letter under the windshield wiper of the van. It smelled like perfume, artfully rendered, and had poems oriented toward the possible future they could've had together. He'd never met somebody like Steve; he had a family and children. This was a *Brokeback Mountain* situation; we just respected it peacefully. Happiness is a rare commodity.

Ironically we had been listening to a tape in the van for a week, The Violent Femmes, and on came "Good Feeling," we just drove on in total fucking silence, nobody said a word.

All of a sudden things started to really pick up for us. We actually started getting tons of press. Magazines like Skyscraper paid attention to us. The whole Providence music scene achieved national recognition for probably the first time ever as a place to play, people wanted to see Fort Thunder and there were so many good bands finally getting on the road, people thought of Providence as a place where good music was finally coming from, so our audiences quadrupled in size. We started being talked about more than that Colombian coke from Pedro.

We were playing Brownies with Black Dice, who were always standoffish towards us. Two of the guys were brothers, they had Dr. Seuss qualities, they were Swedish or something, greasy dudes. But we played with them often. They were hot shit in NY because their RISD class had moved there by this time, and I believe they migrated to Brooklyn also, and were "geniuses." Black Dice was headlining that night. The doorman at Brownies told us that Chloe Sevigny came up and asked, "Did Arab On Radar play yet?" And when he told her we had, she turned around and left. She ended up seeing us at other times and supposedly was a fan. We were highly aroused by this news. It kept us going.

We were far closer to The Pixies than anyone could imagine, internally, we strove for that type of greatness, perhaps a 100 dollar royalty for life from BMI or ASCAP? That was all it was... nothing more, and we loved each other in that gay-love of oneness and togetherness. It mattered not who was on top, we all melded into one, on stage and off and we played naked not for them but for us in our oneness at the time. We played in the boiler room, together, for us.

You are supposed to compose the perfect song, it is 2:42 minutes long, the golden mean of audio and be damn sure you get 8.5 hours of sleep per night as the surgeon general says, eat your tofu and fucking drink that water. Only a handful of people can comprehend much more than that, the shit that is done without adhering to the rules. Only a handful of people, perhaps it is IQ, can enter this elite group of listeners. Some of us have to compensate for life's mishaps, some sort of cocktail to make it through, and G_d bless you if you know what your formula is. But for whatever reason, many different angles we had to listen to, something about what we were doing started making sense to more and more people.

Phillyfest was one show we felt pretty bold about playing. We were excited to meet some new friends and some old ones again. Black Dice played, we knew them from back home. A band I really liked was An Oxygen Auction, they were amazing, a huge dude rolling in barbed wire on the floor, pure noise, which was very popular genre of music at this time. Rachael, the other member, she took a drill, a power drill, perhaps a Dewalt or some Sears brand, and allowed it to chew up her long brown hair, it was painful. We became really good friends at the time. I was happy. The fest, it was at this club Killtime and the guy from Born Against did sound, someone sabotaged us in the name of the Old Guard of Punk, this guy tried cutting our power. Craig ended up smashing his head in with his drumsticks. The guys from

The Locust participated in a micro-brawl that broke out, water bottles were thrown; it was fun times.

We had a lot of violent situations in Philly. We played another show with some Skin Graft bands, this real gutter punk girl assaulted us, Eric was fondling his penis from the stage and she stepped forward and maced his balls. I didn't even know what was going on, he just ran off the stage real fast and through the crowd, into the back of the loft space into the shower, yelping. Steve was already escalating the aggression earlier on by punching a hole in the sheet rock wall of the venue. This was a show we played with Zeek Scheck on the bill. I always loved Rose, she drove off in her mom-mobile station wagon all crazy the next morning. She toured by herself with her equipment. She ended up hitting people and running over garbage cans, backed into a fire hydrant. It was amazing to witness, just a moving meltdown, she illegally sped away yelling and on to the next show I suppose.

Piggy-backing off of the credibility we had established long ago playing those shows with Dropdead, we would still do hardcore shows. On some strange level, we did have it pretty sweet, very few other bands could transcend scenes the way we did, it was an asset and a curse. We landed in DC somehow, playing a punk matinee show, capitalizing on anarchists. Rob had this Shelter tattoo and we never could put it together why he had got that one, he seemed so the opposite, until it was revealed. He'd been boycotting the merch table for about a week and refusing to come out of the van, he'd have us buy him a 6 pack and piss back into the bottles and we'd have to take them out later because he wouldn't leave the van. Somehow he overheard in the parking lot of a show while we were playing that a young woman was in trouble. We got done playing and he came out, to our surprise in an elated mood. He was frantic about telling us we had to drive Xena, a local crust punk, to the hospital. His punk sensibilities had all flooded back and he was more loyal to her in this moment than he was to us. We pieced together that Xena was dumpster diving and she was real hungry and her habit and blah blah blah... she had drank out of a half gallon of milk in some dumpster and thus had food poisoning or worse. It was like a lawn sprinkler coming out of both ends. Rob was like Prince Valliant and insisted that we go immediately. She had already taken off sprawled across the mid-section of some other crusty punk's bike. I recall us driving for miles beside them feebly offering suggestions and help out the window, going about 5 miles an hour, we were like an escort of sorts, shuttling them in safety to the hospital at Rob's command since he was at the helm. Eventually, we came to our senses, sped up, and turned off; hell, vegan slips are a fucking pain in the ass.

The *Soak The Saddle* tour was very different. Andrea had left the band and Craig's father had passed away days before the tour started. When I think of Craig I think of this tour, not the Arab On Radar movie, *Sunshine For Shady People*, not the songs, not the good times or the bad, not even the drumming! I think of this trip out. It was a confused time. I remember going to his dad's funeral, a big Catholic Church, all the brothers, his mother. I felt really bad, but then again, I didn't know what to do or say, no one ever does, so I saved the bullshit clichés and just tried to respect the guy and give him space. That is what I would have wanted. His dad encouraged Craig's interests and at this time it was the band. I think that drove his decision to, days after the funeral, not cancel the shows, just jump in the van and go. We did it, very quietly, not too much "tour joy." I remember the uniform color was green on this one, (we changed Dickies colors for each tour, I demanded this, I was a detail-obsessed nutcase) and Craig duct taped with black gaffer tape a band around his arm signaling he was mourning. I liked that he did that. I remember feeling that these uniforms were important and honorable to us. Our set was only about 20 minutes long. Many of our old friends who came out last saw us playing amateur, long, drawn out weirdness of the *Rough Day at The Orifice* songs. They were quite blown away by the more hard-core, blast beat noise we were doing now, after playing with Dropdead we had some credibility in the hard core scene so many of our shows were split between playing in these college elite sweater-rock scene with bands like The Make Up, Death Cab for Cutie, June of 44, and other pussies and playing either matinee early all ages hard core shows with the likes of Los Crudos, 10,000 Dying Rats, and Dropdead. We thought we had it made on this level, best of both worlds, this had to pay off, it didn't. We just confused both scenes. In hindsight very few bands enjoy respect from both scenes, typically either one or the other rejects the band, besides Men's Recovery Project I can't think of many others, or at least at this time there were none we knew of.

The post show antics on this tour were almost as intense as the on stage performances. We were hurting and angry, probably all grieving something a bit, frustrating lives, bad day jobs waiting for us at home, homelessness, chaos, so we fully lived on the road and our attitude changed. Nihilism took hold, we did a lot of very fun stuff, went places, saw good bands, smoked a lot of pot, and the girls... Craig made a conscious or subconscious decision to have *foreign relations* as often as humanly possible on this tour; I realize now he was seriously grieving and not feeling much in the way of self-esteem, but we weren't either, and apparently many young, very young, and old, and big, and small, and models and moms, and a few grandmothers weren't either. He just loved everything and everyone. We all were chronic masturbators but this experiment he was conducting was outrageous. We could barely find him in the morning, of course we had to leave for the next town and without phones or ways to get a hold of him we had to wait idly for him to be dropped off in some beater car by someone's mom he had been in the company with the night before. It became hilarious of course, at the time we didn't see this as much of a problem, we used to joke about mumus because one lady in the southwest dropped him off and was wearing one and was very large; of course to us this was just an excuse to make fun, be total assholes and relish in our testosterone juices like pigs in mud. So many mumu jokes ensued. Overall, it was innocent, the more devious ones of our band had girlfriends and didn't do their evil on these particular nights.

I want to somehow address the "Song Writing Process." We would come in, set up, talk about our lives for ½ hour always. Smoke pot, or have a beer or two, or not. Then hit record on the 4-track or later the Zoom recorder. We'd jam for hours and hours, usually 6-8 hours, then we'd identify the salient riffs/beats. Next time we'd start with the highlights of those long jams, if early on they were not progressing or suggestions were few we might go back into the chaotic open jam. If something did catch fire, we'd discuss, over-analyze, argue, re-write, re-record, discuss tempo, length, and prominence of certain parts. We whittled out songs from fallen trees. The lyrics were always separate and last to be revealed, not open to discussion, sole ownership with Eric, which was of course, a minor problem. The song titles were derived from really stoned laugh-sessions when weirdly enough brilliance came. We all chipped in to come up with titles. I can only imagine how much better these song lyrics/vocals in general would have been if we subjected them to the democratic, holistic, spiritual process. Thomas Jefferson cried and we settled for narcissistic fascism, it worked, but in my opinion this method was always a compromise and a thorn in the band's side.

We did our homework, knew when to use a big note or two, I had to play with fucking finesse. Truth be told songwriting was a laborious task, two steps forward three steps back, we certainly were editors, directors, like Martin Scorsese or Stanley Kubrick, take 20, 21, 22, 40. But it got right and we knew when to say, "close enough." The songs themselves on our earliest material were post-punk, between *Queen Hygiene II* and *Rough Day at the Orifice*, we had changed a lot, perhaps one portion of the reason Andrea quit. I detuned to a spiritual raga style tuning AAGEE and the structures of the songs became less orthodox. This was about the moment we started gaining confidence. But mommy, there were proper parts enough to keep the sweater-rockers engaged (or at least curiously guessing.) Then there were no-wave parts that even Lydia Lunch would be positive about. We lubricated the songs, gentle, no hard thrusts but crescendos and Wagner-esque endings. We rolled with resistance when needed and were purely confrontational in others. A song such as "Menstruating Thrills" did emotive whispers and we put the moves on all the hot people. We were willing to play and to play the game. Claro, we thought we would be famous like Jesus Lizard level at least, but we were not.

We had hate-lists; chords never, pop structures rare, this made it hard to put vocals on, we probably would have had greater success as an instrumental band, frankly. We were in a pocket, pretending to be somebodies, fathers, lovers, the Keith Richards in France, it was all delusions, but why not, "act as if" as they say in AA.

We had a regular ritual of discussing band business at, let's say, shady locations. "Balloons," the 18+ totally nude strip club down by the waterfront docks was one of them, every so often one of the strippers was actually under 30; but we managed. We planned, schemed, created, thought, and philosophized in this environment. We booked shows from there. We primarily kept each other in the loop about all the nonstop business we were doing all day and night every night and day. When we practiced it was so serious that this business stuff could not be discussed, it was a pride thing, a thing of honor. It was a way to stay close but keeping up the front of importance with each other, and no one interrupted when a person was talking. We all dressed well for these occasions. It was out of respect.

Then there was this one time, perhaps this was more leisure than business, Eric, Craig, and I had a habit of frequenting "peep booths," mostly non-human, just some back room area at various video, dildo, sex shop type places. We went to one Amazing Superstore on Charles Street, very near where we practiced. The clerk held open the velvet curtain and led us back. Each of us got our own booth. I recall vividly watching some straight porn just doing my thing, taking my time, suddenly a hand came under my stall door and strewn across the floor were numerous index cards—just blank index cards, Dewey decimal system shit. I was a bit scared and my cock went down in pressure. But I kept going. I looked across the bench and at my seat there was a 3x3" hole in the wall and in it was an eyeball; he kept making noises at me, hissing, saying, "hey," but not responding when I said, "what." I bent over to pick up a card in the neon light, I felt nervous, and someone knocked on the door. Instead of opening it I reached down and this person took my hand, gently. I opened the door, my fly was still open and my cock was out. They sat next to me and tried to make out. I pushed their face away. We watched some L.A. porn star getting it on with a junkie for about 30 seconds, and then they picked up a card off the floor. Without fully coming back up they grabbed my knees and looked up. I just put my head back and they started sucking my cock. I pulled out without coming in their mouth. The person was a bit surprised and got up real fast and left, slamming the booth door. I didn't even care what they looked like. I smoked a cigarette all 50's style and stared at the hole in the wall, empty, no one watching any more. It could have been one of those guys for all I fuckin' know. Fin.

Randy Hein owned The Living Room, a local legendary space that everyone and their uncle had gone to. Every legendary punk band probably played there. Folklore had it that The Exploited decided to jump over the bar and drink booze from the bottles and Randy beat their asses. Ramones stories of them drinking beer and then pissing into the bottles in the dressing room waiting for some groupie to sip from them. On and on. Eric lived in the same town as Randy; when outside the club he was a model citizen, coached Little League, was a straight up guy. We started hanging around The Living Room because Eric had had Randy as a coach and Randy let Eric and Jen work the door on some nights.

Randy's office inside the club was a wicked hoarding situation, piles of shit up to the ceiling. There would be chairs with boxes piled underneath them, stacks of *Sports Illustrated*, *Playboy*, sound manuals, bills, then a plaque from REM that was given in appreciation when they made it big, all this shit just piled up willy nilly. Of course there was a lot of shady shit going down at this rag tag club. It was real blown out, drop ceilings falling down, rooms just closed off due to random plumbing issues. Every week a guy would come by and go in the office with Randy, one of the very few times I'd see him go in there. Much later when Kevin was the sound guy, I worked there for a stint learning sound. That guy still came every week. He had on new looking clothes, Timberland boots, a flannel shirt, brand new but nothing flashy. He spoke to me once, he said, "here, take this ounce of weed, you sell it, keep the profit and give me 200 bucks, sell it to your friends." I was too scared, I declined, and he just scoffed at me like I was a pussy and said, "all right," then left. He was mob, he was collecting on Randy's gambling debt. Randy was such a kind and giving guy, a Santa Claus type, but everyone has a weakness, sports gambling was his. He leveraged use of the club against debt and these types ran a lot of drugs through there. Grateful Dead cover band night, c'mon, this place was a fucking market place. The Providence police got their envelope too, the gang and the government are no different as Perry Farrell said. We'd all seen what the cops would do. Providence was a violent place, especially at night. Everyone has a story to prove this, like the time my landlord moved in these junkie types, they'd pass out in the stairwell, make noise. I thought they started dealing out of his apartment; he did too. He called his brother who was a detective and very quietly, late at night, about four cop cars rolled up, no lights, nothing. The guy junkie was out but the skinny lady was up there. It was brutal, they punched her in the face, dragged her screaming across the street, put her in the car cuffed and sprayed pepper spray in the car, shut the door. She kicked out the window, they probably killed her later that night, who knows. But, nobody fucked around in Providence. Neighborhoods were quiet. The business of the night went on and no one made a peep. This was just the way it was under Patriarca, then Cianci's time. Tough love, but many do not realize it was this kind of activity that made it possible to have Fort Thunder, lofts, and the scene we had; we benefited from the corruption too. They had no problem at first. No cops came, even though there were 400 people they'd stall on fire inspections. When Buddy started to take a dive, so did Providence. That's when things shut down. They just tragically shut down the best art/music creative space of our time. They wanted to put in something profitable and of course the whole thing failed, even economically speaking only, the city should have embraced the arts. Because that was the force of the appeal, what made it a unique place.

Every Halloween there was a big show at The Living Room. It was a real big deal. Astoveboat had put out their album, *New Bedford*, and Sub Pop had grown interested in signing them. We'd heard through the grapevine that Jonathan Poneman was to be there. We half-cared, it was more about the show. Six Finger Satellite, Dropdead, Lightning Bolt, Astoveboat, us... we played in our tight whitey's a la "menstruating man" t-shirt we had at the time. It was ballistic. 6FS played in baseball uniforms, possibly a throwback to The Warriors? Who the fuck knows? But Rick their drummer played in a KKK uniform and the hood on his head extended upward to a 4' point. It was absurd. They always played a bit too close to racism and anti-Semitism in lyrics, art on the albums, etc. Fucking Catholics...

Astoveboat was not signed, they were muscled into staying on Load in a passive-aggressive way, just like Lightning Bolt. Sony Records offered Lightning Bolt a contract, they declined, good for them. All these major labels were pointless by 2000. It was DIY or Die and Steve Albini did a great interview on all the reasons why labels of this size were just a bad investment all around; we thought, forget about it...

So Eric and Jen would work the door at The Living Room, this club in Providence. I bummed around like a wanna-be at this joint for a long time. Eric and I started booking shows, I recall many a night printing out shit, at this time the internet was very primitive, the dial up modem, those sounds were very similar to the bands we played with at this time, especially the jazz-oriented ones. It seemed like I was on the phone endlessly in these days and Eric was too, he was a real schmoozer and had the gift of gab. I was socially weak and less fun to talk to, but we made a good team because without my creative, far out, freak-ass ideas shit would have gone absolutely nowhere, I give him credit for being game for a lot of it. We worked real hard and to put it in Beatles terms: if he was playing Paul I was happy to play John, we had that type of relationship, one founded on necessity.

We somehow set up a show with The Melvins, rumor had it they were shopping around due to bad blood with Lupo's and The Met from past experiences. Randy green-lighted the gig. We had to come down real early because believe it or not at this time The Melvins had quite a demanding "rider." It was a bit of a *Rocky II* feeling because Randy was so down and out, he had to go to the liquor store daily to buy the booze for the bar that night, no distributor would touch his joint, the place was being used by people who didn't care, outside forces, people he owed gambling debts to, it was a mule operation at this point, he was just waiting for the guys from the Hill to light a match. We got out his silverware and helped set up a chicken buffet, full dinner. We had water in the dressing rooms, everything was a go, despite the ceiling tiles sagging with air-conditioning run-off and the piss smell, the place was ready to rock. From Boston came a call in, around 4 PM, we'd been there cleaning up all day, the call was from Robby Fraser The Melvins' William Morris Company agent. He was debating with Randy whether The Melvins should take a day off or play, telling him they were tired, they were having fun in Boston and might not want to leave unless the show was really good. This guy was just feeling things out and tenderizing the meat. We were in an awkward position because you could tell that many many years ago Randy was done with this type of shit, he had booked all the best of the 70's, 80's and 90's now at this time, you think you are telling this bullshit to someone who hadn't heard it before. Fact is, he was doing this as a favor to us, like a coach, but it was pissing him off to have to deal with it. We cashed in a lot of street points this night. This pussy called back, he had a figure this time, demanding 2 Gs over the already contracted guarantee they had. Arguments ensued, and in the end The Melvins didn't come. King Buzzo prior to playing their show in Atlanta, Georgia, went in the local rag, the music paper, and said that they skipped Providence when asked, and that the owner of the club they were playing didn't support the local music scene, made it seem like no one in town supported them playing the venue, a total fucking lie. Needless to say, we sucked it up, someone scribbled on the chalkboard at the last minute before doors saying, "The Melvins Cancelled." At the time we weren't shit, especially to this stoner-rock crowd, half the people didn't come in. The parking lot was full of sort of tailgating zombies talking to each other about the cancellation, half weeping. It was like Jerry Garcia died or something. We played, but the tone of the night clashed with what we were trying to do, you know, people are already bummed, we were to blame, then we play and antagonize with treble and provoke them musically? It just didn't happen, we stood pretty still, played our set with minimal theatrics, took the beating. I did get pretty vocal about discouraging people from attending their next show 2 years later; a few friends had joined The Melvins for this tour and they got real mad/confused with me about why I was doing this. I tried to explain to them and the city, but might makes right, popularity is hard-wired biology, we were small primates and they had the testosterone, so they won the argument. This is how the Music Industry really works. After the party on Halloween our next show was playing with Anal Cunt, Seth Putnam was nutcase but we were psyched to play with them, Seth was smoking a lot of crack at this time, I remember these dick-fucks showing up with no equipment, and they threw a two-year-old temper tantrum because they couldn't find anyone who would let them use their gear. We were fine with it, we didn't give a fuck at this point, but it was us intimidating them a bit. They carried on being whiny bitches but we had respect for them. They played a great set and we talked about playing together more often. But honestly, we really wanted to play for normal people, we liked women and we preferred to play in a more well-rounded audience. The angry dudes in trench coats shit, we had no use for that Columbine shit. They liked it though and we respected that. If you ever doubt their integrity I can say that one time we played the night *after* they did at a club in Detroit once, the ceiling fan was hanging down from one frail wire when we arrived. Apparently the night before Seth had thrown a cinder block at it taking it down. They trashed the fucking place. These guys were cool, then Seth died as most crackheads do, and that was that.

Fort Thunder was an amazing place, in through the parking lot, Dunkin Donuts on your right, all the way back. The door was on the ground level, an inconspicuous door to a mill. If you were really insane, once shows started, you could go up the rickety rusted fire escape staircase inside left right, the stairs made creaking sounds reminiscent of an old boat, the sound only old wood could make. Then on the left was the door to enter. A wonderlust of art from the miniscule to the large hung everywhere, it was an installation in itself, posters, bikes, stickers, GI Joe figures, lots of Legos. Right when you walked in there was a narrow corridor, prior to it opening up to the full loft. This is where Ben McOsker or Brinkman would be sitting in the hall with a large plastic Halloween pumpkin or sometimes just a beer box collecting donations. People would throw in some cash. I always contributed, stupid fuck I was, but it was an ethics thing, people who don't support shit on this level can go fuck themselves. The irony of this mill building, where the oil soaked into the wood floors, blood, labor, sweat, toil of the poorest, now was that it was occupied by the elite's kids going to the best art schools in the world and their Ivy League friends. This was not in my thoughts much back then though. Regardless, it was usually a magical night, better than Studio 54 I'd bet, more creatively-motivated than The Factory at times. I dressed the part. I knew everyone at the time, we all knew each other, respected each other's work, challenged each other to do better, to progress, and to think. I remember seeing Doo Rag, Harry Pussy, Le Tigre, all sorts of amazing acts night after night, this was my whole life at this time.

You know that guy who freaked out in a certain psychotic way, he always showed up, all of this was going on, it was great. People were peacocking at all times; on display. Weasel played in Misty Martinez's band, it might have been the same show as To Live and Shave in LA, but she played Fort Thunder. Liz Armstrong was in her personae as Misty Martinez, this was the night when she began her set dancing scantily clad, really sexy actually. Xander threw a full beer bottle of beer at her when Misty played; this situation was quite awkward. No one agreed with this type of rage and violence at this time. People were shocked, not a cool outburst. Feminism has always struggled with understanding submissive female roles, perceived, acted, or real. Liz used to host dildo parties for lesbians in Chicago and went on to be a huge feminist writer for many magazines. Read some Kathy Acker for fuck's sake. Similarly, there was this time someone thought it would be cute to spray the crowd with water from the fire extinguisher, climbed up on the scaffolding they had set up in there, and sprayed everyone, but of course it was ABC Dry chemical, a flame retardant powder which suffocated people in the room. People freaked and had to be carried out. I never saw the person who did that again in Providence, I feel bad about that, it was a mistake and they were just unlucky. But this ignorance was rampant at the time, too much privilege... This is why people are hierarchical, there is no other way with us electro-chemical blobs.

I had this cassette tape alarm clock when I lived in a loft, I lived in this place adjacent to Fort Thunder that was called 556, the only tape I could find was a Doors Greatest Hits one, so every morning I would wake up to what I rewound to the night before. Over and over, day after day, it was always "Love Street," you would think this would be something nice to wake up to, an affirmation to start off the morning, positive vibes and meeting everyone later in the day thinking about their best days and forgiving their flaws, if it may not have been one of those best days on *this* particular day. But, no, it enraged me, I don't even give a fuck, whatever sound or noise or anything whatsoever I can blame anything on is my mortal enemy if it wakes me up. I feel that there is no greater punishment than to wake up a person who you know is enjoying sleep; that is truly a crime. Mr. Mojo Risin' did not get me going that early in the morning, I just needed coffee and a bowl of Honey Nut Cheerios and I was good to face another day of coin showers at rest stops, moist cat chow for pillows and smoking hash off of beer cans...

The Safari Lounge was an unlikely venue to be cracked but somehow Ben McOsker broke that scene. Jimmy and his wife ran the place with the snake, an albino ball python; he had in an elaborate tank in the club. Jimmy was a very old Puerto Rican, he hunched over like an ogre, he wore this really rad leather hat, almost like Slash from Guns and Roses, but more of a derby than a top hat. Interesting fact, if you pay very close attention to the scenery in the video game *Grand Theft Auto 5*, some art fuck must have jacked this bar scene and co-opted it into the game, you can't miss it, the albino snake, the layout is a wholesale model of Safaris. If I ever find out who the pencil-necked geek is who stole this for that game, I will ram a pool stick up his or her fucking ass, but I digress... Many a sick soul would talk about the nights where he would feed the damn snake, I heard rumors of multiple mice, rats and a few times a rabbit, it made you not have an appetite for the pickled eggs that sat on the bar which may have been there since Kennedy was shot. By the time we came to be accepted in this bar the place had digressed to a homeless hangout, there was nothing left. Major drugs passed through the place, usually hardcore shit, dope, coke and speed. I regretfully had a few nights where I got really high in this venue. Many people lost their souls here. Ironically, these beautiful RISD students, ladies we called Louise, and Jenny, we all did drugs. Louise was the most hardcore I can think of, she would live at this place, amongst the homeless, something was wrong. Jenny got a job there bartending. I remember spending many nights in there. Jimmy would laugh as from across the bar some lost soul grandmother-figure would lift her sweatshirt up and flash a tit that looked like a deflated football at me. He thought that was funny shit. Shows here were the best I have ever seen, no rules, no limits. I recall Dan St. Jacques, when playing with Landed, an amazing Providence band, hanging from the drain pipe of the ceiling like a baboon in heat. My personal favorite Providence band ever, Astoveboat, played there one night, to virtually no one, me and about 4 heads, and 20 homeless moss-gathering chumps. It was amazing, their theme, "nautical," after their legitimate roots in New Bedford, Massachusetts, a traditional whaling town. Astoveboat was two guys Tom (a Portuguese maniac) and Dale. Dale was in a great early 90's band Glazed Baby who had promise in the Jesus Lizard scene of yesteryear. Astoveboat was not famous, but the music they made was legendary, Dale played a 50 gallon steel oil drum with bass drum heads grafted to it, a snare, hi hat, and a ride cymbal. Tom had a sick Traynor bass cabinet and some really high-powered amp. This given night they came out with a recording of Morse code playing loud, a fog machine puffing clouds into Safaris, masking the audience, they wore Navy pea coats and looked like sea captains. Blasting into bombastic songs I was totally floored. I remember degeneracy. It was a rough place from beginning to end, but we were royalty there and the place felt comfortable always. It was the last stop late at night no matter where you were in the city.

I felt tough when I went to Safaris. I started making money for the club and with that came respect, not only for the Arab On Radar shit but because I was a Providence local, in and out. Jimmy used to say, "The Arab!" and down a long bar, perhaps 30 feet, slid a shot of Jagermeister, not a drop was spilled. He must have learned this somewhere, an old bartender trick, and we'd toast with a wink and a nod. Business was good, the town was alive, and we were where it was at on that night. I didn't want to be anywhere else. I loved Providence so much. We in Arab On Radar would tout it as a badge. We put it on the map. At first the national circuit laughed about our ocean town. But after us, and Lightning Bolt, Pink and Brown, Astoveboat, 6FS, Landed, Dropdead, Black Dice, etc, we made them pay attention. I liked our local scene. It was the best. We had a microcosm of New York galleries and Burning Man all in our laps, and local heroes were built up, local heroes were torn down. It was pure creativity.

Everyone jerks off to CBGB's bathroom legends but there were many such places that were equally intimidating when you really had to pinch a loaf. The toilet in Safaris was punk as fuck, vomit, spit, drugs, so many people did so many drugs on that toilet bowl lid. I remember going in with an acquaintance and she just razor bladed the top of it. We did a line of jizz, coke, heroin, who knows what, just the sloppy seconds or thirds, zip, up the nostril and to the brain, so gross... This reminds me of the story of how another uncle of mine went to this bar in the early 1970s. It was non-white, a strictly Puerto Rican bar. He told me that he had ordered a beer, the bartender took a pint glass from a local homeless drunkard seated at the bar, rinsed it in the dirty water bucket (toilet water) and poured him a glass. He left. My uncle used to sell "black beauties" and "yellow jackets" pills outside for a few nights before he was jumped and robbed, the place always had a protectionist policy. I was proud to be on Jimmy's good side. To him, I brought in the college kids, money, buyers, and bitches to his place and at the time I agreed it was a *Breaking Bad* relationship we had. When these connected Italian lawyers ran him out and Safaris closed, I was really depressed. Months later I saw Jimmy and his wife and the snake huddled into a little car driving, and I cried.

I'd get these "guilty pleasures" bands going on every once in a great while, interests not consistent with our music, music scene, taste, or any standard relatable. I suppose it started with loving *Annie: The Musical* in third grade and that horrid old bag of a teacher Ms. Lareau making fun of me. But over the years there were others on the back burner. Extreme. I loved Extreme for some reason, while the rest of my musical repertoire was pretty metal, Voivod, Raven, Celtic Frost...While on tour for *Soak the Saddle* I watched the Troma movie *Tromeo and Juliet*, starring Jane Jensen. I guess I became obsessed and looked up her info on Myspace (at the time it was legitimate) to find that she played music, very safe music, not underground but for people who think they are underground, Tom Waits fan types. I wrote her and she responded to me as anyone famous would to a fan. We were playing a 3-nighter in Jersey, then Brooklyn and on to Manhattan at the Knitting Factory, actually it was the horrid closet in the basement called the "Alter-knit." We were in full testosterone angst mode musically at this time, scary people to be around, actually... I wrote Jane and told her about the show, begging her to come, real poetry from some sappy place. I played her CD on the way to New York, and was laughed at and mistrusted as a result. They thought I'd lost it. I was obsessed with talking about her to the guys, trying to make them see what I saw in the music, someone going for it. Success by an underdog, Annie! That archetype remained. They disagreed. So we played, it was totally over, we went to the bar, her and like 6 steampunk looking girls and guys, her entourage, came from across the room, and I saw her from way across the room while we were drinking at the end of the bar, I didn't have the chutzpah to go up to her, I kept begging Eric to just go up to her and tell her who we were. She was looking around nervously, biting her nails. He kept saying, "Just go up to her and talk to her and say hi," but I just shut down, I couldn't do it. I was 100 percent certain she came to see us that night. I blew it out my ass in a total fail situation. I think I got off on feeling this way during these times. This was a personal low.

Chapter 13 – Bluegrass Graduate

We tried to "make it," "get signed," so many times in so
many ways I'm not sure you could imagine. We'd
randomly send our demo tape everywhere: radio
stations, labels, records stores, so many, hundreds and
hundreds. Funny enough, we did get a response from
our tape sent to Alternative Tentacles. Jello wrote us
back a nice letter saying they weren't actively looking for
anyone to sign but that they appreciated us sending it,
yadda yadda. This boosted our confidence a little bit,
kudos to him or whomever he delegated the task to, for
helping out each and every little guy, or was he enabling
bad music by this effort? You decide. We sent Skin Graft
everything we could, a begging, humiliating letter that
went unanswered. Even funnier is once we were signed
to Skin Graft, Mark Fischer dug up that letter and we all
laughed at it. By dug up I mean literally. Our first stop to
Skin Graft headquarters was amazing, a huge loft in
Chicago with desks and record store style shelves full of
their releases. Clocks with every time zone on them; this
was a working office/compound. Out of the roof was a
huge water tower, an old one, straight out of Upton
Sinclair's nightmare, that one. Mark showed us this
room, a closet of sorts with an eight-foot pile of demo
tapes, just on the floor and up, raked up like leaves. He
said this was years of foliage. So much, and who knows
what was in it, why bother in the face of this pile. He was
so kind, he said take whatever you want from our
catalog and we all shopped like kids in a candy store. Of
course I found some dank box with one or two 7"
records from the earliest stuff and he let me take one,
there were only one or two there, the rarest, dustiest

stuff. He was so laid back. Then we discussed business. He was too fair, no contract, 50/50, he just loved the music. He was a patron and he loved comics. I feel bad that we were so pompous to insist on our own artwork, but we had slaved for too long, we had Fort Thunder as our artists and always stuck with them, too aged, too seasoned. It would have been nice to have an old school release with the comic from Mark and Rob Syers (Gumballhead the Cat), we were arrogant and entitled. We wanted our own artwork, we were a second-wave Skin Graft band, all but disconnected from Mt. Shasta, Ruins, Zeni Geva, even US Maple. That scene was awesome and it was sad it started to end as we were coming in. Fuck. We became great friends with Mark all the same. He was a really classy dude, always looked good and added to our weirdness. I wish we had been more sane... I felt like someone had our back always. Mark joined us on a European tour when he moved there; it was an interesting trip. We met up in some ancient room, white chalky walls, with thin transparent light bulbs lit in chandeliers hanging from the ceiling of this chateau.

Long road trips...one time we drove from Salt Lake City to Seattle, almost 30 hours, way past the mandatory rest time for professional truckers. Truck stop love, showers paying with quarters, someone looking at my ass and me looking at them, pondering, "Is this life?" Truck stop love eating a stack of chocolate donuts and white milk, my chosen sustenance. Just chewing that shit up, making a slush in my mouth of these two items, feeling like I was needing vitamins, needing protein all the time. Once you drive and drive and drive you get the lime green delirium. One time we were in Michigan and our house host was impressed by us. He tried to reciprocate, looking at our next destination, he encouraged us to go out, live, experience life, go over the longest suspension bridge in the world and enjoy the "U.P.," short for Upper Peninsula of Michigan. We accepted his adventure, how fun it sounded! At sunset we hit the bridge, exhausted, 50% impressed. Time went on and on. We drove in shifts. I recall frustration when consulting the map at how easy it would have been to just drive boringly to our destination. Nothing was learned, nothing was experienced, no events warranting a tattoo, quite the opposite, we lashed out at each other. Total survival mode, do not go near my dog bowl or I'll snap at you. Time went on, it was 3 am, Craig was driving, I remember riding shotgun and being fucking pissed. He was too tired to drive. We pulled over to gas up, cold, see-your-breath chill in the air causing vibration. We got on the road again, my head fell back in petit-mort. I recall waking up to a slight screech, swerving on the road. Before us were a mother bear and three cubs crossing the road. We were so far out. The van almost overturned, speaker cabs smashing in the back. We just looked at each other and laughed, many jokes about Goldilocks and fucking Goldicocks ensued. Sometimes near death keeps you alive.

Playing at the Fireside Bowl was like playing the Taj Mahal of our kind of music. Selling merch on the street outside of Fireside, we just pulled up our van and hung our shit off the side of it, prior to the show people would come up to our gypsy wagon and buy whatever knick knacks we had for sale on that tour. Somewhere, in someone's basement or perhaps their record shelf their lies some very rare Arab On Radar material, mostly in the city of Chicago and by these methods this is how it got there. It was during this time we ended up sleeping in parks, many parks, on the ground, like the people you see. It pains me to recall it, so I will leave it at that.

Our friend Brian Peterson's place was a refuge, he had an apartment with a bunch of punks, we shared many blunts, he had a band, Vietnam. The punk house was real chill and he was a real chill dude. He showed us around Chicago, the comic stores, the record stores, all the best people. We got to know these cool folks in 90 Day Men and a whole jazz-influenced scene.

We sort of enjoyed playing with US Maple a few times, they would show up late, real late to play, they would make us wait, and wait. I think they were buying snow. At the time we told ourselves that they showed up late because they knew we'd own them, this is how inflated our egos were.

There were bands we did not feel that way at all about, no competition whatsoever, just mutual respect, one was 7000 Dying Rats, we played with them, again, due to an irrational connection to the hardcore scene, but G_d it was fun. Playing at those Fireside Bowl matinee shows, and late shows, it was the heart of humanity at this time, it was always the most fun.

There was this strange night in Chicago, at The Empty Bottle playing with Ruins from Japan. James Iha from Smashing Pumpkins came and watched all the bands. It was an Asian alliance thing I thought at the time. Many hours later, when the bartender looked tired, I sat drinking, shit beer after shit beer, until all the drink tickets were gone and far beyond. Near the taps there was this lady. She had on a leather jacket, her hair was Hitler-esque. She looked a bit fascist, but honest too. We started talking and it all progressed so quickly. I took the van from our very sweet front parking spot and drove her around the side of some mill building adjacent to the club. I was impotent but eventually she was in the driver's side riding away. Apparently hours had gone by, perhaps it was 3 or 4 am, James Iha was long gone. We were fucking away in the dark but suddenly headlights illuminated us in the worst way possible. No mistaking what we were doing, all naked and riding. It was those guys. They borrowed the sound guy's car to go look for me and boy were they pissed. She laughed and said, "Let them watch." We had talked a lot earlier. She was a paralegal for a famous Chicago attorney. She had to work early (like one hour from then), so she said goodbye. The walk of shame ensued. I gave her the number of where we were staying and made promises to stay in touch. Eric had a poetry reading at Quimby's the next day and I invited her, she said she'd come. I constantly encouraged Eric to be a poet, I wholeheartedly believed in his work, I loved his poetry and his lyrics were the best. Thax Douglas was there, he wrote a poem for Eric, they had a weird relationship those two. My acquaintance didn't show up, even though we fucked to four or five Kate Bush songs the night before. I was sad. I was so tired. After the readings I went back to Brian's house and crashed hard. The rest of those guys went bowling. Frantic calls to the house were made, many voice messages left while I slept because I guess my lover was at the bowling alley and they tried to get me to come down. I slept through it all. Some things were not meant to be. It was just too sad, too psychologically draining. I felt like a cheap date and hated myself, my body, and my work. I decided to never go back, it was a lesser form of love, one of self-hate and an impossible, longing, aching sensation. I did not feel whole, I felt halved. I kept going.

We were in the middle of nowhere then we came upon our next destination, Minnesota. We stayed with all sorts of odd characters in these days, just loafing with folks who had very little to do with the music scene. Andrea knew a girl, perhaps her college roommate, who had subsequently gotten married to this guy Doug. I think this lady had some sort of relationship with Andrea in college but I can't say with absolute certainty, college gals are always in some sort of relationship. Doug was a professor at a local university, he studied Geology, the dude dug rocks. This fascinated me because I knew nothing about fucking rocks. He told us a few things about chipping techniques and minerals and places he travelled. We all went to Dinkytown, where Bob Dylan hit his musical puberty. It was great looking out over the river at the place my Jewish hero had done all the legendry stuff. This is how we lived, off of the mercy of others, teachers are the ones who faithfully plant the seed, in boring brown dirt they drop a boring brown nugget, but they know the tree that will grow and bring beauty into the world with its blossom.

We voyaged on to other areas in Minneapolis, playing at the "Purple Rain club," First Avenue and 7th St Entry a huge venue, it was anti-climactic, later on in the night, very much later we ended up going to Prince's new club, killer DJ Black guy dressed in all brown suit smoking a brown cigar cigarette, just killing it on the turntables, everyone else was Black and in high rolling suits, we rolled in White in our AOR uniforms, very smelly… we sat around for a while drinking beers and that was it. Somewhere in the mix of this mess the next day we met Nick Sakes of The Dazzling Killmen fame, folklore legends; Roman used to tell us about the super fun cookouts Nick had with Steve Albini and The Jesus Lizard, etc.; there was no cookout for us, he seemed very tired, like he needed a nap or was on Lorazapam or some shit. He let us stay but he also let us down. He was always at the right place at the right time, but we were at his house, which for us was the right time but the wrong place. We should've just driven back to Chicago.

Arab On Radar

Date	City, State		Venue
8/10/01	Philadelphia	PA	Rotunda
8/11/01	wilkinsburg	PA	Mr. Roboto Project
8/12/01	Chicago	IL	EMPTY BOTTLE
8/13/01	Chicago	IL	FIRESIDE BOWL
8/14/01	Iowa City	IA	GABES OASIS
8/15/01	Minneapolis	MN	7th St Entrance
8/16/01	Omaha	NE	the Junction
8/17/01	Denver	CO	15th Street Tavern
8/18/01	Salt Lake City	UT	Kilby Court
8/19/01	Seattle	WA	Graceland
8/20/01	Portland	OR	Meow Meow
8/21/01	San Francisco	CA	Bottom of the Hill
8/22/01	Los Angeles	CA	Knitting Factory
8/23/01	La Jolla	CA,	CHE CAFE
8/24/01	Phoenix	AZ	Modified
8/25/01	El Paso	TX	Cantina La Tuya
8/26/01	Denton	TX	Rubber Gloves
8/27/01	Houston	TX	Notsuoh
8/28/01	New Orleans	LA	Mermaid Lounge
8/29/01	Atlanta	GA	Star Community bar
8/30/01	Greensboro	NC	Onion Cellar
8/31/01	Carrboro	NC	Go! Rehearsal Studio
9/1/01	Baltimore	MD	Otto Bar
9/2/01	Brooklyn	NY	Northsix

Mike Apichella of Baltimore, his house was insanity. Never slept on such cold tile flooring before in my life, it was like a walk-in freezer and I was a Blueberry Pie. But Baltimore always was a special place, it was the city where we felt most at home and could relax. We played the Ottobar almost every time and we loved it. Nice little stage, long bar, and this great dressing room upstairs that had a window open over the street, it was like our favorite hotel in the Catskills. I always remember JP from The Locust saying John Waters from *Pink Flamingos* fame would come out to see them and that they were friends. Eggs, Eggs, Eggs... Edie would have cried. We'd subtly hint that he should tell Waters to check us out, thinking he'd love us too. It was always, "Yeah man, he said he will try to make it." Regardless we were always on the John Waters sighting hunt, "Is he in the back of the club...?" No, he never came. He didn't, many didn't, we were too "hot" for them like hot potatoes. We would rock the balls off this club's ass and I hope that people on those nights enjoyed it because we were all in for you 100% in Baltimore always... We'd get really high on weed and play sets we rarely played. We had such great fans, they knew our music, we felt obliged to give them a good show. We'd usually stay with Mike Apichella in the early days, this guy was a mensch, a real mensch.

We became friends with Celebration, a band whose members used to be in Jaks, a band on 31G Records that we absolutely adored for years. They were like The Birthday Party, goth rock. They were so elegant and their place was everything you'd dream it to be. I could just imagine the BDSM sessions they had, oh my, it was obvious. They had a coffin in their apartment that we thought was fucking awesome. You could just imagine what happened in that thing. Such fun people! Of course, we all lusted after Katrina, steaming sweat, but we respected the relationship status and also the fact that to her we were the Three Stooges, Curly *and* Shemp era.

That time of the band was when I was fully immersed, 100 percent, lived it, these songs just kept ringing in my head all of the time and I couldn't even be a normal person. I was a vegetarian at this time and when you're on the road for so long you lose respect for other people's normal routine. I knew places I would stop at I would never ever be at again, so there was a sense of entitlement there. I would walk into Burger Kings and tell them to make me a cheeseburger, just don't put the burger on it, which would scramble their brains and derail their entire slaughterhouse process but they would do it, and they wouldn't know what to charge me. I was happy to pay full price eating my bun with ketchup and cheese in the band, I remember thinking, "I really get things my way these days," and that came with a cost. I could never get too deep with people. I always had one foot out the door, but there were times when I tried to be romantic and to feel some emotions of love or caring.

I had a special friend in Baltimore, we had romantic late nights right out of a Woody Allen movie, I pushed her around in a shopping cart at the empty store parking lot at 3 am, just laughing at the full moon. I think she could understand my situation. You know, "throw your homework onto the fire, come out and find the one you love." We'd go to cafes and have hot coffee and peach pie late at night, until the sun came up. There was no future in this but it really felt good in the moment when it took place. I wish I had just left it at that. She came to Providence and I ruined everything; at home I found it hard to cope. I was shell-shocked, but that was no excuse for being so awful in my natural element. My apartment was boring; I had no job. I was lazy and I basically was just squatting at a place that had nothing to do with me whatsoever, it was just down time and I didn't even know what to do with that time, it wasn't productive, this state of limbo made me probably as uncomfortable as she was. And I'm sorry for that.

Something about Baltimore, does Love shine brighter there? Maybe it was a hyper-pheromone zone? Steve's girlfriend in Baltimore was cool, she brought him flowers on stage. He must have had a great time, we had to go get him the morning after, like seriously rip him off the mattress on the floor of her den and drag him out of the house; he was pissed but we had to get to next town. We had to extract that motherfucker. Once again, the Ottobar in Baltimore, Maryland; it was in John Waters' fruitcake neighborhood.

PCP Roadblock was this band who brought total insanity. We played with them sometimes in Baltimore. We played with them too many times in their hometown of Richmond, VA. Their vibe was real GG Allin level shit. The road was full of assholes who had cashed in their chips a long time ago; people best to be avoided. PCP Roadblock were real psychopathic types, we played with them a lot, smoked pot, had parties. I remember one show where one of the guys said, "hey everybody," and we all looked up to where his voice was coming from, he was up on the roof of the club pissing golden rain off the building on everyone, just spraying away. He just pissed on these girls who were talking to us near our van. At the time this was funny in theory, but the piss was not funny. Total destruction. We usually stayed with Sam McPheeters of Men's Recovery Project, he had no furniture with the exception of a mattress on the floor and a bookcase with many Nazi history books, *Mein Kampf, The Rise and Fall of the Third Reich* and shit, that was odd. He seemed totally lost living in Virginia. I thought he was some sort of fascist for some reason at the time, which he was not; maybe he was doing research or something? I realize how much cooler he was to us than we were to him back then, I mean, why else would he put us up? He was just a cool dude regardless of his fetishes.

We met with some lovely ladies in this town. This all sounds so righteous, honestly there were many times, not only here, where the clothes hit the floor with people we met. We said we'd get naked, and then it was revealed by just how many articles came off in which way; I remember the belt, fast through the loops flickering like a machine, the shirt goes up like a curtain, pants drop like a shade. Thrown socks, not folded or placed. Panties came off, wet, nights of erotic kissing and sweat. Lights on, heat like the jungle, gambling heat. Climaxing, setting records, total revelation, thinking and emoting, we did these numbers. Then it was done, the whole fucking thing was over.

We did stay at these bona fide Nazi's house once in Delaware of all places, they were about 21 and had just gotten out of the Army on furlough or something, they were Skinheads through and through, they had an Irish flag on one wall of their unfurnished shithole apartment and a Nazi flag on the other. They wanted to party, they kept us up all damn night. Romping around

Sieg Hieling and acting all tough, which they were, they were ripped physically. We just practiced our tolerance skills, we had nowhere else to go. Delaware was so weird, we played this café attached to a hotel in desolate no man's land. Ironically, Jonathan Richman played there seemingly every other week, what a nut, it was like a retirement community, no one was younger than 50 and most were 70 and up. They clapped, nice nice, but this was a weird zone. People showed the Love. Although this partying with us was another road occurrence, people wanting to "sleep with the band," not sexually, just to lay down next to us, all sprawled out party style, I can't tell you how many fucking times this happened. It became on on-going joke... Many people did just curl up next to me, I'd wake up being spooned by some Charles Manson looking motherfucker and just roll over and pack my shit up and leave, it didn't even phase me, Helter Skelter, so what?

On and on we travelled, we played in Denver, Colorado, I think. Upstairs at a bar you knew cool things happened at, but just not on the night we performed. It was a bridge show, one that took us more north than south on the route west. Drinks, load in, we were "head-lining" per our general contract, but you'd think if anyone cared they'd save it for places where people cared about such things. But no. Chugging on and on they played, Neil Young-ish song after Young-ish song. "I am so sorry, I dun you wrong," when in fact you were playing video games, nothing romantic about that. Droning, on and on, it was now one twenty am. I think they played the entire B-side to *Rust Never Sleeps*. Everyone was gone. People who came to see us at nine, faces saddened hour and hour until a puke or a pregnancy situation seemed to usher them by us, basset hound eyes, they waited and waited, I felt bad for them having to put on such a performance. These cunts "Slipstream" played on a Thursday. The drummer did sound Tuesdays and Wednesdays. They were the house band. They got done, then did the thing where they just left all of the gear on stage, walked off, went to the bar, and got laid or lit. Total meathead universe. Steve was most mad, we discussed getting on stage, he was apeshit. He went up and started throwing their gear off the stage. He threw a Fender Twin off of a three-foot stage, bam. The drummer, a young chap, came up and starting breaking down his shit. But the elders, crusty barnacles of the dock and the slimy rope women that hung off them, no. We played, tone deaf to anything but our music. Thanking an audience of ghosts; no one dressed up. The rain came, a downpour, sheets of rain. We drank until 3 am. Drink tickets. Really late. Loading out was down a long wooden staircase. Down, down, like a typical VFW Hall. Maybe 50 stairs or more straight down. I was carrying a speaker cab with Steve, and *vvvip*! Smash, crystallization! Steve's forearm was bleeding, blood dripping off the elbow and spattering on to the wall of the stairwell. I looked up the crevasse of stairs into a bright light. They stood there. These drunk fucks had thrown a pint glass down at us. I was showered in beer. Steve put the amp down while I launched into a tirade about death, Neil Young, respect, and more threats. It got formal! Load out then let's finish business. By 2 minutes everyone was informed on our crew. Rain, rain, we were soaked, sneakers drenched. Every time we passed each other while loading out the threats got thicker. "Bitch," "Fuck you," "You are dead."

This got so serious. Eric grabbed a bike lock we used to lock our doors together in the van in crazier cities, but we needed it now in this madness. This became a real situation like *The Outsiders*, some Ponyboy shit. We lined up like the British. No one said anything but hands were up. Lightning flashed and thunder crashed in the background. We could barely hear what we were yelling at each other over the downpour. I said something like, "you want to talk shit or you want to!" and the next thing I know, I saw red and launched forward real impulsively, my fist connected with a snap to his jaw without knowing what the other guys were going to do or if this was really happening, but it was. Violence ensued, the mayhem came, and a complete bar room brawl broke out. Steve and another guy in Slipstream bowed back. Rob, Craig, and Eric brawled it out with these fucking mongrels. Slapping sounds, choking sounds in the mud, on and on we fought bareknuckle. I can't imagine what the Civil War was like. Vulgar gurgles and wind being knocked out of people's lungs were all I could hear. I went to the ground with the biggest anushole in Slipstream, scraping my knuckles and rolling on top of him. There was a pothole about three feet wide filled with water. Somehow I remembered a Gracie Jiu Jitsu move, miraculously, and held his face in that water. I heard that bike lock hitting people in the head, the pinging sound of it bouncing off their skulls and bones. Sounds of flesh and meat being hit rang out. Thud, thud, thud, kidneys being pummeled. I didn't realize his face was under water and I was blacked out, probably almost killed this guy, I know I was trying to. Out of nowhere a complete silence came over the situation. Craig pulled me up off of this wheezing bagpipe. We got in the van and sped off, leaving choking, blood, and mayhem in our wake. In the van I was soaking wet and the rainwater mixed with blood dripped off my hands and elbow. We all were panting, trying to catch our breath. Then we all starting laughing really loud at what had just happened, going, "holy shit." We always found a way to get at some form of entertainment, be it musically or otherwise.

It seemed like two or three hours later, the sun was up, it was probably 8 am by this time. I was in a posh vegan café, eating tofu scramble and drinking organic coffee. Some guy with a ponytail who looked like a yoga instructor, and his girlfriend who wore a pseudo-leotard, stared at us. They came up and told us off royally. They said, "You beat up Slipstream! *Why* did you do that?" and told of how they were local heroes, helping with shows, nice guys who helped the scene, innocents. We just left. I had acted like an idiot. But I must say it all goes back to the playground. Steve was low in the pecking order because he was a very non-violent person, he just didn't want to get involved ever. But Eric, Craig, and Rob, and probably worst of all myself, were people who came from a certain place and couldn't help ourselves. We never started shit but we definitely finished it. An insult to one was an insult to all, where we were coming from. We had no qualms about using violence if someone was messing with one of our crew. Say whatever you want about it, but that's the way it was.

Chapter 15 – As Gold As Mold

We needed a new chapter, and thank G_d one came. We had moved into our new practice space, a massive floor of my grandfather's building above the garage of his well-drilling company. He let us practice there but it always had to be late at night, 7 pm - 2 am was a typical practice. We played three nights a week for many years this way. We always saw each other. Down at "The Space" we wrote most of our best music (*Soak the Saddle* up to the end). We had big plans of building a small recording studio and I dove into trying to learn all that, but to this day I am an amateur. We set up these fake walls, paper thin, just tacking up wood paneling on the walls. It was pretty cool. We had plenty of room. It had this rickety old landing made of steel girder, we'd play on and on for hours then go stand out way up high in this thing in the summer, in the winter. We could park our blue van down in the back in its own spot. The garage doors opened up to load in real easy. We'd smoke a lot of grass up in there, always leaving joints laying around, my grandfather would find them and bitch us out, "g_d damn potheads" he'd say; we were...

We wrote *Soak the Saddle* up in here. It was an intense spurt. There were these little mice that lived up in there, so cute, they'd scurry around, really neat little beings. I think the music freaked them the fuck out, like a huge cat was going to kill them, they scurried like they were in a psychological experiment getting shocked. It was a cool place, very conducive to musical creation. We had the opportunity to relax and had 24/7 access, we'd stay there until 4 AM sometimes, just playing and playing, it was all we wanted to do. Some great shit came out of this dedication and excruciating process. We always talked a lot about music and what we wanted to do and there was this bravado where if you played some shit it was almost embarrassing, our egos were huge at this time, we didn't play much shit music. We never fucked around with normal music, we had this pride where we really felt as if we were doing something very very important, that we were John Coltrane or Albert Ayler, we were in our own world we created and we took it severely seriously. It was a matter of self-respect and high respect for each other. Of all losses, it was not the end of playing music with these guys that hurt, it was that they quit feeling this way, we were goodfellas until they became dishonorable drunks and drug addicts in rehabs and mental hospitals, a big no no in our world, a sign of unacceptable weakness, this destroyed our legacy.

I knew the story the old guys used to tell about "when poverty comes in at the door, love flies out of the window." People thought I was crazy, a control freak, possessive. How can you not be possessive of your music, your creations that you worked so many hours on, developed such a personal connection with, maintained a relationship? These weren't people, these were ideas we were responsible for. This is a digression. The real root cause was simple; for right or wrong I held a humble opinion: don't tear down an idea that someone, not necessarily me, came up with and put on the table without immediately offering it with a better idea or an alternative (well thought-out, worked on) that is valid of consideration and discussion. Try living life with that belief, the road has potholes. Feelings were hurt, mine included along the way. We were emotional people, schizoid flavors, core positions in sadness and confusion industries. But we had goals, dark goals.

We were in Joshua Tree and I'd never been there before. We got in around 5 pm, set up tents, ate well, camping. I recall the sunset, shooting stars zipping by in the sky, a real fireworks show of meteor showers. I walked out stark naked and all alone, far out in the desert, nude, I finally relaxed enough to be horny and with a throbbing erection I stood there looking up, warm air blowing on my ass. I just whacked off. When I got back, they were like, "where were you," so I told them the truth thinking they'd give it a try, it was that good. But they just thought it was a white trash move, and it was.

I have no idea how it happened but we ended up in Los Angeles on the *Yahweh Or The Highway* tour when we were doing pretty well, playing mostly sold out shows to 200 or 300 people, we played at The Smell in L.A., a DIY venue with good people running it. We played a pretty good show, all the antics, dancing, hyped show. All sorts of people were at the after-party that spontaneously happened after the bands were done. We were sitting around smoking pot and indulging in alcohol, beers mostly. Just remember me saying that safety is the main issue. Then again, this fog rolled in an entourage of rich, hot people, the center of which was comedian Andy Dick. He was at his prime at this time, a schmaltzy weird guy who had mastered sarcasm and biting insults on his audience, he probably had his own show somewhere I am not sure. He was fun, manic, probably on coke and asking for more. We bullshitted for a bit, it was amazing the women who came up and asked him stupid shit the whole time, just barraged with fans.

We did a little rudy toot toot together, his not mine. He got really hyped up like a Chihuahua and was prancing around, just moving around the whole time, he was a real star, someone who was always like this that was obvious, a fun guy. We laughed a lot, many jokes about The Smell and what caused the name and if there were indeed unresolved plumbing issues. Things were going so awesome, when he got up to go piss or something he was so hyper he just licked the side of my head and ear, like how my parent's Chihuahua thanks me for feeding it crackers during the holidays. He was like the dog whisperer. It was so much fun. Somehow I started talking about his comedy, a wee bit too loud, and I probably got a wee bit too high, I made a comparison which escalated into a rant about how he'd co-opted Tom Green's whole personae and shtick, he laughed at first, then he got really fucking mad, talking even faster and faster, then he stormed off, unlike a cloud, more like a triggered madman. I had a horrid trait of finding that no-go button, like a child I pushed it at the wrong times. Daddy was pissed and he pushed me off his lap. The party continued, I was swimming in his runoff. It was a stormy night all around.

Chapter 16 – Spokesmen for Schopenhauer

Once we got to the West Coast with the *Yahweh* tour, it was funny how different regions of the country had different tastes in music, all these nations... We'd definitely be in the top 10, the show we played in Seattle with The Locust, The Blood Brothers, Subtonix, was one of the largest shows we've ever played, three thousand plus people in attendance. It was one of those shows where we played and there were faces as far as you could see with furled eyebrows and mouths agape. There was no "roar of the crowd," rather strange sounds like nobody was talking to each other, maybe they weren't even enjoying themselves. It was more struggling aimlessly to find a reference point for what was going on. All it took was one complimentary declaration from The Locust or The Blood Brothers to be accepted, but there were moments where people were trying to figure out what we were all about, and some of them got it. All sorts of fun characters came out to see us play, Joe Preston was one, he was a cool guy, definitely did things his own way. We sat at the bars and drank. We were never involved with heavy drug use, the pot and the booze did the trick. Once we got out there on the West Coast we could tell people were into getting fucked up on a whole other level. We knew each other so well, we were a family, so when someone went off the rails the rest of us would intervene like older brothers, this was another thing I think went the way of the Dodo when we stopped caring. We limped through these shows and kept the wind in our sails, kissing the Southern Cross as we did our late night cruising.

1. #5
2. cocaine mommy
3. vatican self tabut aqua
4. rivers for a stone
5. Birth Control Blues
6. God is DAP
7. My mind is a matter

Olympia, Washington was at the heart of PC mentality. When we were out there we again passed some sort of safety check and by association we were allowed to play. It was all a mistake. We were walking to the gig and some chicken fight broke out between JP and some local dude; they ended up purposely messing up each other's hair, some type of bitch fighting in Olympia. I am sorry but this is just not what we were habituated to. Back home you never fucked with another person unless you were really prepared that it may end up with your life on the line. People are cold, but at the same time, far less insults are exchanged. If you messed up back home and started shit with someone you shouldn't have you could end up dead. We just watched this episode out there in awe, like, when is someone going to stab? But I guess it is more civil to stay within the circle of non-violence and safety. How these people achieved that, if they did, I cannot understand.

At the behest of Brian Peterson and Justin Pearson we wooed shows and ended up playing with the Blood Brothers. Cody, Jordan, Johnny, I recall that their drummer was on probation or some shit, for some unknown charge, it seemed absurd to us, just looking at the guy we were thinking what the fuck could this skinny dude have done? They had gone balls deep into the major label indie label seriousness zone, they had this punk ass bitch tour manager who thought he could tell them what to do all the time, "fix your hair Johnny," and then he had the gall to try to tell us how to backline our equipment. We straightened this guy out real fast, we didn't play that shit. It had a sad side, everything was on loan from some fuck in a high rise in LA I am sure, their

Orange amplifiers, rented. They had it out to be the next Nirvana. I made real friendships and I think we provided a well-deserved respite from this delusion some rich fuck came up with, predictably while on coke, in some LA party somewhere. G_d, fuck that shit. Half of the band were hired guns who we never associated with, the other, real passionate artists who just got caught up in it all. Of all of those dudes Jordan was the most righteous guy, I met his sister who was also very cool; he came out years later to see Made in Mexico. I consider that guy a brother, a blood brother for real.

Hanging out, we had a fucking great show, we played a huge venue with The Locust and The Blood Brothers, perhaps one of our biggest volume of people shows ever. The show we played was straight out of *Less Than Zero*; it was where I became a superior human, an uber-mensch. I talked away, had fun, bitch-slapped a few punk ass bitches and was on my way, totally high, an ass.

Again, some kid came by and messed up Justin's hair and we were ready to pounce but he had some hand slapping spat with the kid, these people were weaklings. They just passed each other in the street and then all this beta fighting broke out, again it was like 2 hens in a chicken coop, feathers flying everywhere. It was cotton fuckin' candy all sticky but sweet, non-threatening. That night, some of The Locust crew broke into some guy's house apparently and trashed/stole his record collection, it was some vendetta for some slight against a female in the scene, some accusatory shit, I would imagine anger over hair products, gel and the like... This was bitch-ass pussy fighting and it lacked honor, it was the first time I'd seen this be acceptable, I was sincerely shocked, it was not the way it was back home, I wasn't entirely sure I could have these guy's backs. All this hair fluffing and trash talking like some gossiping grandmas at a nursing home, real sneaky and weak, what kind of people were these? We were in the vanguard for such insanity and it spread nationwide, they think this is progress, I call it meaningless, it is the death of Art and Freedom of Speech and Due Process and it is partially responsible for the death of the music scene we played in for Christ's sake. How are we to think? How are we to eat? No one cares about either anymore. Death, dead, dying, Calvin Johnson...

Although, honestly, this after-party was a remarkable event. We went up about 4 flights of stairs in a glass-encased stairwell to some sort of rooftop party situation. I really feel like "mashed yeast" was on the menu here. There were probably 500 people up there, shoulder-to-shoulder, talking loud, dark ambiance. I had a few conversations and probably twice as many drinks/tokes of marijuana. Out of the darkness an arm came up at my face, I grabbed the sleeve and it was a leather jacket, somebody's key to their bike lock or house or something was about three inches from the tip of my nose. Everything was in some David Lynch situation with blue lights. I snorted a humongous line of blow off of their house key. Then I really had great conversations and made all sorts of plans to do all sorts of crazy shit. Probably everybody in that whole room I said something to, like "nice tie," or "you look like you're enjoying yourself." It felt good but I didn't feel like many people understood entirely what was going on, myself included.

On or around this same time we put out a stellar

7" with The Locust. The design: shit, cum, piss, puke and snot - colored accordingly - brown, white, yellow, purple and green. It went over well, Neil Burke from Men's Recovery Project did some of our art; it was a great contribution to the World, whether or not the World knew it. I was proud of that shit and for the first time, I felt like I had not let myself or this band down.

The music kept getting further and further out there. There were phases, epochs, that were all like evolutions in the Big Bang. By the end with songs like "Running for Asthma," we were so far gone. I'm not sure people can follow us there. It is out there where Jandek lived, beyond. It was a product of years of listening to nothing but ourselves and loving our own produced music. We were alive and our music was our language. We didn't do too much talking then, we had reached enlightenment. I can't recall much, but around this time we bounced all around the vast United States; from place to place we played to our best abilities.

One time we were playing in Wisconsin, first taste of fear of police and serious police brutality, the cops there were straight up fascists, the Germans, etc. All our hosts talked about was their cheese, good cheese and how much they liked cheese, and avoiding the cops. We wanted to fight the police but they assured us this was a bad idea. This was a brown-shirt situation, one that is all too common in the US of A. We played, peacefully, then got the fuck out of there. Free Wisconsin!

Staying in Cedar Falls, Iowa, I recall playing with Vida Blue, our buddy Joel Anderson's band. Joel was a cool dude who helped us out a lot over the years. He was such a mellow soul. We had great shows here with him over the years, Joel is family. One whacky-ass situation was when Craig sat up 24 hours on a swinging bench with a 15-year-old girl, all night on a porch, something out of *Little House on the Prairie*. He was still collecting data for some marathon experiment he was conducting. And lets just say, the results were as predicted.

Playing Arizona, long dark straight highway. I needed some milk so I was going into a convenience store, I'll never forget this Kid Rock looking dude in Daisy Duke shorts, no shirt or shoes but off his belt a Colt Python hanging, he had no teeth in, forgot the dentures or something, we are not in Kansas anymore Toto... But it was cool, he got his beer and I got some chocolate donuts with white milk and all was right with the world.

After playing at The Bug Jar in Rochester, NY, we met some friends: a cool dude, really handsome, and his girlfriend and a female friend of theirs. They offered to put us up at their house. We happily accepted. We went in and upstairs in their house to what was an open loft. The entire room was made to look Roman: vines, all white, Roman paintings and faux sculptures. This was the place they called, "The Treehouse." They told us they had kind of a bachelor party type of situation the night before and that this was why all the blow-up dolls and stuff were all over the place. The story didn't quite add up for some reason but we didn't care. It became obvious that they were swingers and this place could have been a porn set. It was awesome. We partied, getting quite inebriated. Michelle, Kurt's girlfriend, kept whispering to him and looking around at us. This progressed to her saying, "*Please Daddy*," and him glancing back at her shaking his head, "No." Whining a bit she said, *"Please, Daddy, I'll keep my panties on."* She was really horny, it seemed. Who knows what may occur next, we thought. He kept glaring around at the room and staring at her, saying, "not with these guys." Admittedly, we looked like criminal-minded people and they hadn't known us for more than an hour or two. The friend of this couple sat down on the white loveseat with me. I said really dumb shit like, "I really like your hair," and stuff about the band lifestyle of sleeping on the floors at people's houses. Minutes later I looked back at her and she was blowing one of the blow-up dolls and looking right at me. Total eye contact, we were locked in. I was speechless and aroused. So much biology kicked in, real fast. She came right up to my face and sat grinding on me cowgirl style.

She said, "You look pretty high, you probably don't even remember my name."

I said, "Pftt, of course I do."

"Well, what is it?"

"T'huh, c'mon…"

"What is it?" she persisted.

I said dryly, "You know I know your name, Michelle."

She just huffed and exhaled a long, long, breath, got up and walked away, over to the other side of the coliseum table like a lion that just ripped a Christian's head off. I looked over at Kurt's girlfriend and said, "But… you are… Michelle. Okay. So then… So that would make you…um, Kelly. Yeah. Got it now." I tried to apologize and get back in the sexual sparring like a gladiator, but that was a circus disaster that had a tragic ending. I was categorically less than a little brother at this point. I ruined the overall vibe big time and buzz-killed the whole situation. People went to bed, lights went off. Some of the people got out their little Sharper Image night lights and started reading another chapter in the David Foster Wallace novels they brought in their luggage, resting in their sleeping bags, it couldn't have been more stale in this room now. I tried to ask about partying onward and someone shushed me like a librarian. That was it. A day later with a wicked erection in the van I thought of how much could have potentially happened. That was a personal low for me. But we hung out with Kurt and Michelle just about every time we went to Rochester, that was our go-to place, another home away from home. How the fucking hell did I give Caligula blue balls? The story of this band, the story of my life...

We'd definitely compare our shows, reflect, "let's jam it like Brooklyn," or, "the best show so far was Baltimore." We rated this not only on how well we played per se, but sometimes on how the show unfolded, did we have dancers, did we fight, those were funny moves when you gave yourself a wedgie and hung your ass from it on the coat rack on the side of the stage just dangling there like a bird house. Sometimes we punched out the songs hard and got real serious, others it was the Marx brothers routine, we were so fucking bored but at those shows people usually got another type of performance. There were sub-themes to those as well: "Erotic Night," where grotesque Tracy Pew style hip gyrations ensued or, "Joke Night," where idiotic stunts were tried. I remember bending over, putting the headstock of my guitar down on the stage, then bending my body back into a *Dirty Dancing* lift type of thing up and over the guitar with my stomach resting on the butt of the guitar. Freestyle guitaring. I'd break guitar cords almost every other night until I sought out the "L" jack ones and just duct taped that to the guitar. We'd play the songs almost exactly off of the record, we rarely ever improvised a note. We loved the free-jazz but we never got there, we wanted to and that was where it was heading but the wind direction changed, mackerel sky, advisory warnings were given.

We had many good times with The Locust. We played a sold out show at the Knitting Factory in NY, Manhattan; there was still human life there then. 3000 people and probably 500 more crammed in. Total riot. This situation occurred that only people that have performed live probably could really understand. We set up our gear and once we got out on the stage my amp immediately malfunctioned. It must have been a fuse blown, or something else. It took the wind out of our sails completely and shame and blame were flying in all directions, from the audience, from the band, from the sound people. It was a panicked situation. I had been through this probably a hundred times before but this particular night I threw a complete temper tantrum, a "hissy fit" as we would call it, on stage. Someone graciously volunteered their amp, and the sound guy was setting it up for me and I probably shouldn't have been pissed at all. I felt pressured to perform, to live up to our insanity, and I was completely insane at that moment to be honest. I threw my Travis Bean across the stage like a battle-axe. It did two or three rotations high up in the air before smashing into the grand piano on the stage at the Knitting Factory, taking a 3x3" chunk out of this presumably extremely expensive instrument. It dented the headstock of my Travis Bean, which still remains bent to this day. We did manage to play our set pretty well, but my guitar without my natural amp, playing through a distorted amp made the Tweeters overdrive in the most crackling way possible. I sounded like an 80s metal band, Dokken? Or maybe Slayer. But the sound was outrageous and not our style. Ironically people really liked it, we sounded so much more normal this night, like a metal band. They were screaming for more. It's funny how unintended consequences can sometimes randomly work in your favor. We sold so many fucking records at the merch table that night.

Afterward Bobby and Gabe invited us to a bar and we cut out and went. The story was that they knew the bartender and we could all drink for free. It was me and Craig who went with them. We went into a very serious rough trade bar. There were leather men everywhere. They were rough with us, like kids at the playground, their playground, and we were uptown wussies. I had my uniform on so I passed as a fucking fascist from Belgium or something, it suddenly took on a BDSM military look in this context. Bobby hugged his friend and went over to the huge cable wire suspension swing right away. We all laughed and the patrons put dollars in his pants. He took them off after a while of swinging, it was like *Urban Cowboy* at Gillies or something. He had such a smile. He had some underoos on or something, Hulk or Spiderman underwear. He made a few bucks on that swing. We drank a few drinks, warding off desperate men, watchers, idols. I got punched hard by an old guard fucker. He laughed and said I could take it up with him over here, pointing. There was this odd tunnel or passageway that went behind the stage. Bobby took me back there, it was early, the place wasn't crowded yet. Midway back, behind the curtain, in the tunnel, it opened up to a discreet room with little benches, all white walls, and neon green, blue, red, and pink lights. The rug was very dank; it was obvious no one wet-vac'd back here in a while. I sat with Bobby back there for a bit to avoid being punched again. I wanted another adult beverage eventually and everything went back out to the bar. It was so minimal out there, metal tables and barstools, a basic bar, and on a vinyl tarp behind the bar was the word "SPERM" in very big, white letters. I was ready to go, and then I went back to drink up in that room through the tunnel. I felt ugly, stupid, and alone. Nothing was of worth anything tonight regardless of the people.

Arab On Radar was in many ways an exercise in denial. We told ourselves lies and held them close to just about everything we did. A moldy dank basement was a "recording studio," a friend who paid for our recording was a "record label," and the drunk people staggering around the bar (oblivious to us) were "our fans." The bars we were playing in became "venues" for our 3 drunks audience, we performed a "concert." We always magnified the situation bluffing our way through, I was an artist and an author, when if fact I was just a guy collecting welfare and living off the State, a fucking loser. We had an attorney representing us! If fact, it was just some douche bag Brown University grad with that Jeff Mangum bowl cut hair, some guy who saw us open for Les Savvy Fav once and wanted street cred for that. He let us use his name to seem more important and wealthier than we were. It was therapy counseling more than legal. It took years after the fact to realize the narcissistic coping skills I had been brainwashed into believing. These are the beliefs that cults originate from.

People used to ask me about all these fucking bands: Neutral Milk Hotel, Polvo, etc., and I would have to tell them, I don't know what this music is, I don't know where it comes from, I cannot relate to it on any level, I literally do not have these emotions and have never experienced these emotions in my life. I was so emotionless, sincerely to the core of my soul, I searched and there was nothing but the void staring back at me. I was an angry testosterone-laden pervert. My emotions were competition, anger, limbic system rage, reactionary about everything. I wanted to punch Neutral Milk Hotel in the face, not the people in the band, but the songs that represented them. But, the point is, against all odds, this is the exact reason you must believe that you can do things like this, important music, important things in your life.

At the time I really appreciated the lyrics of Arab On Radar written by Eric Paul aka Mr. Potty Mouth our singer. I suppose I coaxed him into the bathroom stall messaging a bit, but he did it. We had a long history of frequenting various peep booths over the years. We would go in, watch porn, masturbate, then leave in a detached way, like lions, no emotion. He wrote pornographic lyrics. We agreed it would be funny and appropriate to scrawl these on the walls of various bathroom stalls in venues we played at. One "stall art" was done in approximately 1999 in the men's room of the Mercury Lounge in NYC. Perhaps this was done out of sheer boredom. There are probably 3 or 4 others out there in the Nation or Western Europe. It was just a perverted way of saying "Hello" to kindred spirits at the times.

1. 3 meAls
   AwAy

2. # 3

3. god is dad

4. birth
   control

5. lurnin for Asth
   blues

6. father, son....

7. my mind
   is a muffler

By the time we started writing *Yahweh Or The Highway*, tensions were tight. You could hear coils over-extending in almost every interaction with each other. Everyone was getting sensitive, like, "where is the pay off for all of this?" So needs of all kinds were met because it took catering to that to keep going. We were getting sick of each other and it became less valuable. *Yahweh* was the last time we could go back at it and it sounds that way. It was odd, the critique process broke down and now it was subtle, passive-aggressive ways that things were written. Craig would get upset about drum tempos being unplayable, too fast, his leg hurt; then he'd go in the bathroom for sometimes over an hour. We would ponder what he was doing in there. I know for a fact I have seen whole rolls of toilet paper full out of the package Pre-Craig, then an empty cardboard tube or two sheets left, Post. Steve and I used to joke that he was "mummifying" himself, like wrapping his body in Charmin's finest and re-enacting some Hollywood scene in the mirror, all sorts of conjecture flew around on this matter, we all had our hypothesis, we used to coax him out, it was a hard process. We would sit out on the metal grates of the fire escape until all hours of the night just talking. All of this was innocent and dealt with as family right up until the time where it was not dealt with as family. We wrote the song "Cocaine Mummy" which is just an argument or a cock-fight put to music, a drowning sensation, panic attack, we water-boarded each other with riffs and beats and nasally whined obscene shouting.

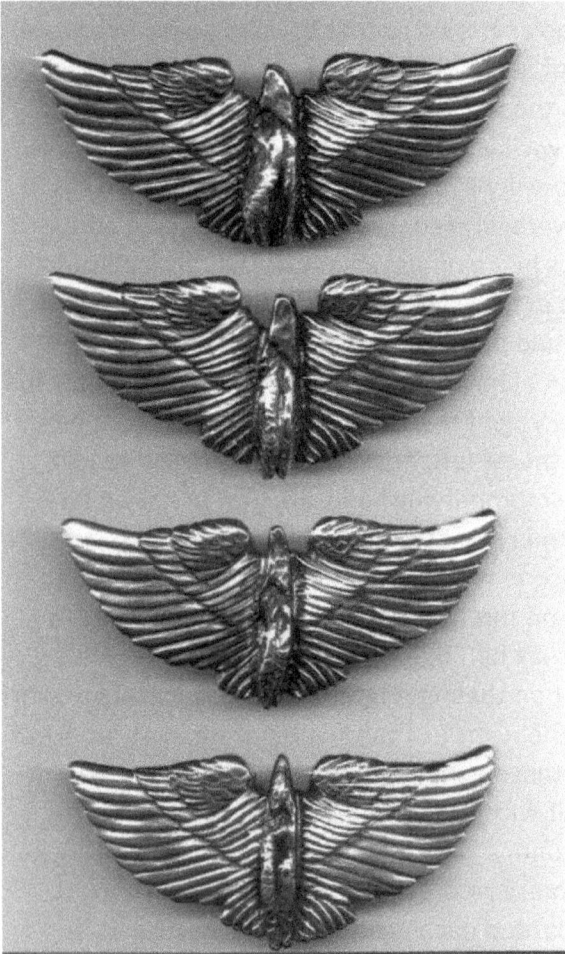

We wrote *Yahweh Or The Highway*, and shortly after we went to Europe. So much planning and cooperation took place prior to us arriving in Europe. Somehow, someone picked us up and delivered us to Joachim, from Sweden. Every once in a millennium there comes along a pure being. I can't recall how it happened, but our first tour of Europe, our first time being in Europe, was with Joachim and his band at the time, Kid Commando. I am not sure he/they even knew of us other than we were a band on Skin Graft Records and as avid listeners/followers of good music we connected. A whole tour ensued but I must mention first that when we played Sweden, Joachim hosted us in the most elegant way, he seemed happy to be back in his homeland. We ate Swedish bread together. Few problems cannot be solved between any peoples over bread, hearty bread. If anyone really upsets you just hand them a baguette.

Anyway, we began our tour flying in to Schiphol in Amsterdam, thinking we were The Beatles, taking our own pictures of the process, knowing not what to expect. We landed in this strange new land and were picked up by Joachim and his pal in a small Euro-van and a rental trailer, the "Einhaagwagon." We had no idea what that meant, it could have said "Fucking Assholes On Board" and we got in this chariot happily. We had far too much gear so some of it had to come in the van with us. But it was a good mindset to be in when we were in Europe. It was relaxing in a weird way. We were met with smiles and Swedish love, all these people in Europe. This is difficult to write about because of all things I feel overwhelmed with love for Europe, I miss everyone so... No pity parties here, we embarked on our first European tour with wind in our sails and youth on our side, there was never a greater feeling in all of my life up until then. I felt complete and satisfied as a person for what I was doing at this time. I walked the streets feeling like I was a musician and nothing more, legitimate and proud, as always there were tales.

Our closest crew was with Kid Commando, who besides Joachim and Johan, consisted of Eric and Eric and Eric, well actually, one Eric was in our band, one in theirs and then their tour manager was Eric too. We travelled with all of these dudes. Often we upset these guys, they spoke three languages, had culture, dressed better, had better taste, had dignity. Meanwhile we smoked pot, and there was nowhere to buy any paraphernalia, no pipes, nothing. We took to smoking hash we bought in Amsterdam off of a beer can. You know you crush it halfway and then make pinholes in the side and if you are real sophisticated you would make a carburetor off the side, and then toke away. We must have seemed like crackheads to these guys. We pissed them off, that Kid Commando.

Yanks within with the United Kingdom, we played in London; the show was odd, but there were a bunch of people, real poodle hooligans, who came that partied down with us. They were very physical, wrestling us while we were playing. The people who promoted the show were extremely British, I remember the girl and the guy, the girl had two swallows tattooed on her shoulder which in sailors' terms was significant of 5000 nautical miles travelled, and she had two, which would be 10,000 nautical miles traveled, which I'm sure she did not do. She was very nice though. Earlier in the day we walked across what seemed to be a park of sorts, some weird hooligans came out from under some shrubbery and started accosting Steve, like, "hey, you want to start shit?" But they stayed at a distance, it was really weird how these people behaved, they were basically taunting us, like little ninnies. They didn't realize when we decided to fight it might mean the end of your life. We played a pretty decent show that night, but sadly we weren't Melt Banana or US Maple, people were standoffish. We went back to a flat in what seemed to be a suburban neighborhood. In the morning we were awoken by some bloke, a neighbor informing us that our van had been broken into; we didn't bother to load into this house because the neighborhood seemed so safe. Some fucking hooligans had smashed out the rear window of our van and taken both Steve and my Tweeter cabinets and some miscellaneous drums. We considered it lost but the people who let us stay thought we might possibly be able to reclaim our items somehow. Craig was extremely upset and as time ticked by, well past tea time, we got tired of waiting so we got in the van and drove around the area. We stopped at a local playground down the street where older teenagers were swinging on the swings, which were obviously set up for 6-year-olds. These juvenile delinquents were just hanging around being bad. Craig ran across the playground and started yelling at an older male teenager, perhaps 15 years old or so, the kids were talking shit back to us in a heavy British accent. The situation got tense. I remember Craig pushing one of the kids, which in England was shocking. These children assed out and scattered everywhere. Moments later some angry parents came up to us in the playground, quite upset. We stood arguing like Parliament with them about the stolen equipment because it seemed like they knew what had happened. After all the violence from our side was removed from the equation, the bobby walked with a goofy teenager back over to the park. Craig was using psychological techniques on them, and he said we were important government officials and just as he said that, a helicopter came up over the tree line, these kids shat in their knickers, and their parents did too, these goofy ass cops came up with yellow construction bibs on like they were going to fix a pothole or something, bobbies, bobbies, these poor bastards didn't carry guns or any weapon of any kind, they were like story tellers or something, they promised that they would go talk to the lads involved and went off to do so. Someone, perhaps the 17-year-old with the bobby holding his hand, directed us to a swampy area over the side of an embankment where our speaker cabinets and equipment were thrown in the mud. We proceeded to scream profanities at this child, like, "you fucking stupid fuck, we're going to kill your fucking stupid ass." And the bobby spoke into the kid's ear, "now they don't mean that, son, they are just Americans, don't worry, lad." Then we parted ways. The bobbies picked up their cones and left. We had some mud and rubbish on our gear but we got over it. Things were different here.

We were stressed because sometime before our show in Leads or some fucking shit, somebody had arranged a meeting with Mute Records. You could tell it was them right when we entered the pub, really well groomed Romulans giggling at a table. I was so out of it, we all sat at another table across the room from them. We got into a micro argument about whether or not it was a good idea to even talk to these people, which boiled down to me refusing to talk with them, but Eric went over and sat with them at their table. To this day I am not sure what was said over there, but one thing was clear, they were not interested in us whatsoever. I feel bad because I somehow blamed Eric for this at the time, but it was impossible to be what they needed and they weren't willing to make the investment in something so wild as our show that night. They had no idea if we could write a song, they did not know our music and the risk was just too great.

We played in Scotland once, we were fucking starving and again the person who wanted to sleep with the band glommed on to us, attached himself to us like a fucking octopus. He decided to cook us a traditional Scottish dish, and I'm sorry, but it literally tasted like an ice cream scoop of rice on a plate, a quarter cup of Alpo's dog food, microwave for 45 seconds, then one teaspoon of Texas Pete's hot sauce, voilà! I choked this shit down and slept on the floor of his kitchen. They pack everything into these fucking little flats. One room had a dishwasher, washing machine, dryer, refrigerator, stove; it was so compact. The next day he told us there was a veggie burger restaurant two blocks down from his house; we couldn't help but feel resentful about this fact.

We took the Chunnel from England to France and maybe it was some sick joke but they give you these little Union jack flags prior to getting on your fucking voyage. We showed up in France waving these flags. People were pretty fucking pissed and we had no idea why.

Sandwiches in France, egg, pickles, ham and mayo, Beouf or Ouef or something gross sounding like that. I swear to G_d I ate that every fucking day. Lyon,

France, our hometown in Europe. Many people think Paris is the mecca of France and we certainly enjoyed the communal eating in Paris, but the best scene for us was in Lyon, actually.

Marie in Lyon... She was told by a friend to come to the club where we were playing. I talked to her afterward and felt guilty, as if bringing her to this place was an inconvenience. There were the nights. We came back a year later and people had thought about what we were going to do and so many more came out to see us. Lyon, France was our European Providence, home but without the perks, a safe haven but not taken as seriously and we would rather play there than anywhere else. It grated on me to keep playing, and just being around those guys all day, seeing the Eiffel Tower miles away and driving by. I think of the brutal depression I was in at times. This is no fault of the band's, or anyone but myself. It was impairing my functioning. I tried to be delightful, giving people what they wanted as listeners. But I listened to other music. We went to a hostel, Craig was my roommate after the show. It was late. I think Craig was on the top bunk and I slept next to Marie in the bottom bunk. We fooled around. I remember Craig looking on, voyeuristically, but there was nothing I could do or say. She was so cool, she started off with us in Rennes and stayed with us all the way to Rome. I basically dumped her there. She said, "You're not going back to France?" I said, no I'm not, and she got on a train, maybe I gave her 20 bucks. I was a fucking dog. I was incommunicado with humans. I was David Foster Wallace in my own way, incapable but productive.

Good shows, this band Gordz played with us but simultaneously hated us, wanted to outdo us, we were eating from their dog bowl apparently. When we played with them in Lyon, they made a major announcement hours before the show that they were going to "blow us off the stage," this was at the last show we did in France, and that they, "had a huge surprise." Time came and then they proceeded to play the exact same set they always played, the only difference was the drummer had on a black cape, to them this was weird and controversial, the cape...

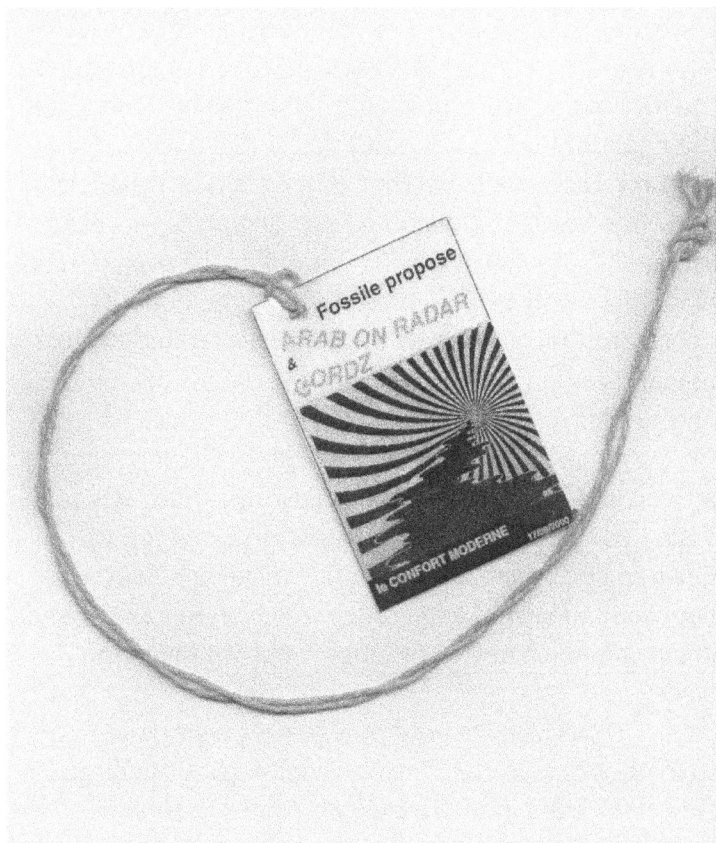

We ended up going to Jim Morrison's grave at Père Lachaise. Everyone else went on and took the rest of the guys to some flea market in France where people of all sorts sell their shit. I stayed back.

I remember in France we had two bad experiences. We parked our Einhagvaggon on a back street, parallel parked way too close and of course our van was locked in between two tiny Smart cars or some Euro-shit cars. Steve pulled out and simply tore the whole bumper off of the car in front of us, there it lay in the middle of the street, some Pierre-ass motherfucker was going to be pissed. I remember looking at Steve who wanted to report this and saying, "Man, just drive the fuck away, don't look back, I don't want to deal with the hours of bureaucratic shit this would entail." He was hesitant, then I yelled at him, and we did just that. We said "bon voyage" and moved on. The place just became too much. Steve was driving out of Paris, we came to a stop, I remember him screaming at the toll booth operator in France "Speak English!!!," as if this guy had to learn our language. We were the ugliest of Americans...

Once we got moving through the countryside and arrived in Belgium, we met this guy Joris. He was a cool dude. As sick as it may seem we were attracted to Belgium due to the prostitution rate being 40 euros as opposed to Holland and France which were much higher. We saw a much better situation here, we loved this place.

Erwin Van Loovehorn was a cat we met in Luxembourg over tea. This guy was a genius in disguise. This night, the bar in the club we played in served absinthe, which was unheard of in the USA, so I indulged. This great DJ in a cut-off Union Jack shirt played all night. I remember dancing and then some odd twitching took over, I was getting into that mindless, walking into walls, zombie state of mind. I miraculously managed to make it to the place we were staying. The place was some sort of "workers' hotel," like a hostel for people working in the area but not residents; this was my understanding. We met these young ladies who did not see our show, but I wished so badly they had, they were all high-end seamstresses who worked for couture lines of clothing. We all left the hostel and went to a local playground, they were worried about some curfew, the town was silent. We smoked our hash; they refused to indulge in such degeneracy, but that didn't stop us. They were interested in staying out later, we made out with them, it was just a matter of finding a partner and pairing up. It was a complete orgy situation but outside in the night and in the sand. For all the wrong reasons we left after this, everyone was tired, and we decided to go get some croissants or anything we could understand that was edible. We were fish out of water and thankful for those who helped us continue on to the byway.

Dennis Typhus was a crazy artist we met in Belgium. We stayed and partied with Dennis, Vinny, and the rest of the crew at what was called "The Conspiracy House." We had another place in the universe to call home. It is funny how few times you can actually relax in these situations, but these guys knew the road and knew the deal and gave us space and respite that we so dearly needed and so deeply treasured. As usual we were pure vulgarians and low class stooges, but they tolerated us and our ignorant ways. Vinny and Joris had a handle on most of the show booking and promotion of this area. They were in proximity to Mark Fischer from our label Skin Graft. Mark had moved to Austria and had networked pretty well to assimilate with the natives of this land.

Germany - The following night we were playing a club with art installation up that could not be removed, it had this very low cardboard ceiling with holes in it at head level, we had to crouch down or tilt our heads to play, which was awkward. We ended up wrecking parts of the installation amidst our performance. Some guy put magic mushrooms, a huge bag, on my amp after the show. It was the season in Germany where the locals would put on their high rubber boots and forage for them, so the bag was huge; we took them. To add insult to injury, we went to this bar, already close to peaking; in the bar was a tight-knit scene, all Asian gents who come out to do karaoke and impersonate to the best of their ability Elvis. None were good, they may have all been Laotian or something. There were Christmas lights all around my head it seemed, even though they were on the ceiling; I'd look away and they'd encompass my head. We walked out of the bar, me first, then Steve and Eric. We came across a commotion going on in the street, a crowd had gathered and two of the Elvis impersonators from Laos were in a brawl over money or some shit. We all stood there watching the fight. Craig was the most fucked up. When he came out, he was oblivious to it all and we sat back in slow motion watching Craig walk right out into the arena of it all. These guys were no joke, and by this point they both had knives out, one guy had been cut, he was bleeding and Craig walked right in between them, we were like, "no, no, no," but he walked into the middle of them, totally aloof, trying to light a cigarette or something. They jabbed around him, he kept looking up. One guy stabbed at his shirt to get to the other guy, then they took off running in opposite directions. We had to tell Craig this later when we all came down. That was some serious fungus. He just wanted to know who had ripped his shirt.

We were such ethnocentric fucks. Europe frustrated us to a degree, at first it was a novelty, seeing so much for the first time. Then we really realized that we were not like them. I went to Germany and thought I'd be welcomed. I remember saying, "I am a Schneider! A tailor, a guy who sewed your clothes, a German!" They were just like, "You are a Jew," and everything took on new meaning. I was depressed as skunked beer. I had an awkward Thanksgiving conversation on that day, of course they didn't have it, but I ended up talking with the local commissar about the Lenin bust that adorned the mantle in this guy's home, about death tolls and all this shit. I talked about what my grandfather did during the War. Odd and scary, good conversation and all, but a body is a body and it doesn't really matter which way the pendulum swung, death is death.

There were many Red Light districts. Most famous was the one in Amsterdam, it was overpopulated and overregulated like the EPA and the DMV had a love-child. I recall thinking, hmm I could go in there, then just as I started stepping a guy went up the stairs, some really fucked up looking dude and I was thinking about how I could not follow this guy's act, no way, no how. It was a frustrating, over-populated tourist trap. Belgium's, as I mentioned, was far less money and far more genuine. The one in Germany was where I got into trouble. On the Reeperbahn there was a Red Light district, neatly organized: there was the black section, gay section, tranny section, and midget alley (only about 10 feet of real estate there). I went up into what was called a "hen house," floor after floor, women behind glass doors enticing every passerby with flashes and offers of all sorts. I was just looking, or so I thought. I chose one woman that looked very French, like "Amelie" sort of, I was very nervous, she had me come in, I was sure I was being watched and I swore there was a guy underneath the bed, I saw his hand pull under as we went towards the bed. There was all this bondage gear, handcuffs on the bed's headboard, mirrors, low lighting. I was very nervous and just wanted to talk, I started spewing out the story of who I was and where I was playing, and making excuses for why I should leave, but she handled my anxiety well, kept me in the moment and put a condom on me. I offered to smoke some of my pot with her, and she accepted, but that seemed only to last 30 seconds and the pressure was back on, leaving me twice as disoriented as I was in the first place. No intercourse but other things, I was in the 69 position when I got off. I paid and she lectured me about how I got more than most and how she felt bad for me but she liked American boys. We parted ways. In my stupor trying to find my way back to the club I actually ran into her again on the street. I begged her for directions but she just repeatedly said, "It's okay honey, it's okay honey," and shuffled by me. There was a big pimp dude, probably Serbian, right behind her so I just left it at that. Those fuckers left me there, they got off faster than I did and ditched me. Bastards. I finally made it back to the venue. It was a show where we were opening for the

Church of the Subgenius, Cult of Bob, which we were really into. They did their whole multimedia presentation and ceremony in my absence. When I finally found my way back we played. Another missed opportunity. I was so late that they went first, then the crowd left after that, and those guys were really fucking mad at me. I felt dejected. It was over. It was totally over. Praise Bob.

It was always a big fucking deal whose shift it was to drive, especially here in Europe. We had a long drive across the Rhineland in Germany, which was going to take hours, and of course it was Steve's turn to drive. We let him do his thing; he gassed up the van and we set out through the wilderness. There are so many holidays I don't even understand that Europeans celebrate, I believe this was on a Sunday, too, and everybody was celebrating some bank holiday, so streets were empty. It was just us, fields, woods, massive forests, and open, rolling countryside. We were pretty happy until this piece of shit Eurowagon kept stalling every time we'd stop and driving all fucked up, which sent Steve spiraling into a minor fit of rage. We came to a complete halt. Totally without trying, the Eurowagon just died. We were fucking pissed. We were so far out in the middle of nowhere we didn't know what to do. Craig, Steve, and Roman decided to walk and seek help. As far as the eye could see there was nothing, except a little dot which seemed to look like a cluster of farmhouses and maybe a church, so far away on the horizon. Off the road they went, just walked straight across the grass in a direct line towards that village. Probably four to five hours went by when they finally returned. The story they came back with was that everyone was drunk in the small village because it was a no-work holiday, no one spoke a word of English, and they took those guys to a local schoolteacher who spoke a few words of English. Craig apparently was the one leading the discussion from our camp. He repeatedly said, "kaput, kaput!" and made explosions gestures with his hands, which really freaked these Germans out; they thought we were going to blow them up, or something was going to blow up, they couldn't understand his retarded sign language. Finally, they came back with two of the dudes in a truck and luckily they towed our van back with them. Someone we called translated over the phone for us, it might have been Mark Fischer's wife, and the villagers told us something that should have been obvious but wasn't, that Steve had filled the Eurowagon full of unleaded gasoline, but the engine was diesel, everyone knew that, which sent the Rage to Mach 10 levels. Our concerns and aggravation were met with total defensiveness and hostility as usual. I forget how the fuck we even got out of there, but I think someone just brought us another van, and someone else just returned that one to the rental place in Munich. The only problem with the new Eurovan was that it was about half the size of the last one. I remember stacking the amps and speakers in the van so that my head was engulfed completely on all sides. Where the window would be was a guitar case, so my head was in a one foot box basically with no light for up to 3 or 4 hours of driving, like a controlled study in an Orgone Accumulater. It really fucked with my brain. That deprivation got to me after a while. To best imagine it just take a shoe box and hold it up to your face, now go on like that for hours on end. Trying to hear a radio through a cardboard shroud was rough. There were phases of panic and sweaty freakouts, but somehow we made it wherever we were going; I had no idea, I was in solitary confinement.

We had a choice between going to Octoberfest in Munich or the more somber choice of going to Dachau Concentration Camp. I passionately goaded the band into going to Dachau. I was back in my zealous pursuit like I had been in Waco, TX, and got pretty aggressive in my lobbying efforts. Dachau is just a normal town, totally innocent, out in the German countryside. We had to park somewhere far away and take the train, which we were not accustomed to riding. We stopped at a beautiful countryside stop and the conductor said something in German about Dachau; as we looked out the windows we didn't see much of anything so we kept going on the train. At the next stop we realized we'd gone past it, so we got out and got back on another train going the other direction and got off at the stop where they said "Dachau." There was really nothing there but over the river and through the woods we found an unassuming sign that said "Dachau Concentration Camp," which matched our map. Once we got into the lobby I looked to my right and saw a guy about my age with two small young girls, probably 7 or 8, the little girl had a red umbrella. But the father had an extremely expensive letter jacket with an air-brushed Apache helicopter firing missiles on his back, it read, "Peace Through Superior Firepower," which I found extremely offensive to be wearing in a place like this. At the time I was part of the radical Left, and of course he was American. I almost started a fight with this guy for not understanding the connection to this place. It was downpour raining. We all felt deep despair, going from room to room where humans were slaughtered, reading every minute detail about what had taken place here. It was a totally depressing, hopeless, suicidal place and we witnessed every detail of it. The guys in the band and Mark Fischer who was traveling with us at the time were really fucking pissed, we could've been drinking beers in Munich with Saint Pauli girl maidens clanking steins and smiling from ear to ear, but instead, yet again, I had led them into the bowels of humanity's worst elements. I still think to this day that we all needed to see this and my judgment was correct in the big picture. I feel that I am a better person for deciding to face this.

On our way into Berlin it was no joke. The Swedes were nervous about our pot-smoking habits. We saw some poor bastard get pulled over by the Polizei. They swarmed the vehicle with about six white and green motorcycles corralling him on all sides; this scared us so we ditched our contraband. Berlin was not a place to fuck around with the police. All of these people seemed like they had the genetics of the uber-mensch and we looked like mongrels from a dog pound. But they were purebreds. We saw the Berlin Wall remnants. The sky was gray. Everything felt like perpetual Fall, dark, cold, gray. This was my impression of Germany.

We arrived at our destination, The Squat. The Squat at this time was not an "iconic autonomous space," it was a shithole. I remember the doors being barred and us having to climb up one aluminum ladder, in through a window, then down another aluminum ladder. Believe it or not, we loaded in this way.

We played to the Black Flag crowd. They didn't know us, didn't know our music, we could have been banging a drum and playing kazoos for all they cared. It was "let's make party fun time Euro Style." Afterward, we were all butt-hurt because our inflated martyr egos demanded respect. So this show was a write-off as most of the hardcore shows we did were, or so we felt at the time. We just left our shit set up, because who gives a fuck, watered down spaghetti sauce and noodles was our pay, the girls looked like extras from Road Warrior, the guys were lost souls on heroin or glue. We couldn't dumpster dive enough shit to ever make this make sense. Who lives like this? Where are their fucking parents for fuck's sake?

A few stragglers stayed around, perhaps they lived there. In a squat I guess it is wherever you sleep, you shit, so who knows. A funny little person came in the proximity of our shit and began sitting on Craig's drums, pitter-patter, then on to full beats just thrashing away. We were pretty stoned, half naked, ready to crash for the night, but I think Craig snapped. He went into his 200 product+ medical, powder, band-aide, aspirin, whatever the fuck roll-out kit, and got his Johnson and Johnson's baby powder. He stormed over to the area we played in and violently threw this Michael Stipe-looking crust punk off his drum stool, maybe slapped him a few times, and took back his throne. With this circle of punk zombies gathered around him he dumped the entire baby powder bottle over his own head, consequently all over the drums too. He angrily drummed for a while which whipped up a dustbowl of talc, a real *Grapes of Wrath* situation like Oklahoma in the 1930s. The room was cloudy for hours later but the place smelled damn good for one brief moment. He really performed well, leaving choking gutter-punks gasping for more. He made them appreciate clean things and fresh air and taught them to stop dwelling in filth. It was chemical warfare at its finest. This whole Biblical escapade had lasted hours. Then like Tom Joad he laid back down and went to sleep, Craig had gotten things done.

Poland was cold. There were rumors of these Nazis, apparently they came to innocent punk rock shows like the ones we were playing to reek havoc all the time. Somebody warned us about this and we were oblivious, acting like we'd take on the whole Reich if we had to; but this was not a Slapshot show in Boston, this was really real and we didn't care. Everything went well and went off without a hitch, but according to locals, we had got lucky. Fucking fascists at it again, be it Left of Right these fringe elements sucked and I feel real bad for the poor souls who had to endure it, for what, to have a good time? The ghost of Woodie Guthrie hung heavy in the air, this guitar smashed fascists…. Fuck fascists.

We had to sit at the border for many hours coming into Slovenia. We were exasperated and tired. This was the show where we played at the same time the Slovenian Men's Rowing Team was competing in the Olympics. No big deal to us, but I guess Slovenia had never won anything so to them it was important. People missed our set, they were not ready for us to play, so when the rowing subsided and they won all hell broke loose. Anything would have done, but tonight we were the entertainment, so we were forced, by *force*, to stay on stage and play. We played our set 3 times in succession I believe. Finally they freed us. People were edgy, I went outside to the parking lot, we were way the hell out in the middle of nowhere, the lot was nothing more than a field near this bar we played at. I was used to hanging out, smoking some pot with people, socializing. A group of lads were huddled in a circle far out in the lot. I walked out and started bullshitting with them to the best of my ability. These guys were rough looking. They were talking about getting back from fighting, which I thought was an ancient situation. All I recall is the one skinny dude from inside who booked us, a mere second before I took a hit off of these guys' weed bowl, just grabbed me by my shirt collar and pulled me backwards across the lot. Once inside, I was like, "what the fuck dude?" He calmly told me that those guys were Serbs and they literally just got back from war, what they were smoking was a very serious drug they called *yaba* (not the Burroughs shit). It was something, he said, I would have been high for about 3 days later if I had smoked it. Some sort of PCP type shit these lost souls indulged in frequently to forget the world. Very scary, I think I thanked him for sparing me the brain damage, but probably not.

We returned to our host family's house where we were staying. It was a beautiful holistic small hut. I remember a woman lived there alone, she didn't say much to us, just cooked and let us go to sleep. We found ourselves eating fresh pears she went right out to the tree and picked and this amazing risotto thing she made with a sour cheese taste and freshly picked mushrooms from her back yard. It was so good, possibly the best meal I have ever eaten. I may have just been grateful to be alive at that house in Slovenia.

We ended up sitting at the border in Croatia for hours. Changing of the guard, they made us take out all of our equipment, every last toothbrush was taken out of the van. Time stood still, listening to nothing, no one else crossing, for hours, just out there, with two comrades waiting. We waited until they verified our documents. The second shift person put it through. It was Rambo III at its worst. I had homicidal visions, but they had the automatic firearms, we had some ham sandwiches with egg on top with a dash of mayonnaise, no contest. We entered the city of Zagreb soon after they took their shits and read their poems in the hot sun. We loaded everything back in (which ironically we wanted to do anyway, and the Tetris formation around my head was superior to the previous one) and went on our way.

Zagreb, Croatia, was a haze, a sepia tone to the whole place, beautiful architecture. We'd just stop at stop lights and grandmas would run up to the car trying to sell us loaves of bread. We arrived at the metal gate which surrounded the local radio station/music venue/cultural center, the poster from this show was sweet, it said we were a "fucked up Pavement," which I guess was true. Everything seemed so Communist there, State supervised. But once the sun went down there was freedom. Freedom in the darkness. We played a really awesome show. Ines and I were compatible. Sadly for me the planets were not aligned, the phase I was in was not interesting. I needed to figure things out, talk, I just needed a break from everything, and somehow she was in the same place. We had such great conversations and I built such a strong caring for this person. I never tried any monkey business with her, and she bonded with me on some spiritual level. We went out after the show, me, Eric, her and her best friend. Eric took a liking to her friend who told us she was 15 years old. Later that night, many small shacks that served alcohol had cropped up along the shoreline of a massive river in the town.

People partied down there, many folks all enjoying the night and the party situation that ensued after hours. We sat drinking for a while and Eric went off on his own with Ines' friend. We sat up all night talking about Life, what the hell it all meant and what the hell the future would bring. That's all I want to say about that.

Vienna – We walked around, confused. Cobble stone streets and old houses, metal barriers piled in the corner of some important square, waiting to be folded out the next day at noon as to deflect the students once again. It was a novelty act. Someday a real storm is going to happen here again, you can just feel it. We rambled up to the museum, which had for the first time on display, "Freud's couch." It was all in the papers back home. We ran up the hallways, up the stairs, no line, surprisingly. A girl with indie sensibilities greeted us at the entrance to Freud's chair. She explained that we were too late, the exhibit had closed 1 hour ago. We begged and begged and this super cool person let us have access after hours to the couch, I remember laying on it thinking of *mother*. We thanked her on the way out. It was one of those things, Jung would have approved, people were short in those days.

In Venice, Italy we stayed with the sweetest guy, a local promoter named Tiziano. "Si, Si, Si," was his answer to everything. He lived on his family's farm approximately 20 minutes from Venice. He was very stressed by us, we whined about not having a proper (English) breakfast, this poor guy got up at 5 AM and made us pasta, thinking we wanted to eat, none of us touched it. We were exhausted. He told us the last band to stay with him was Nirvana and that Kurt Cobain liked his leather jacket so much that he bought it from him, to give to Courtney. Lo and behold, Courtney was wearing it in the Hole videos and live often. He was so happy about this, totally ecstatic, he devoted much time to listening and worshiping Nirvana. Kurt had offed himself by this time. All I could think when sleeping on the mattress on the floor in the upstairs of his farmhouse was that Kurt's head was on this pillow and he had laid in this bed. Maybe he even shot up right here where I was sleeping. I wasn't even stoned on pot... it was a long insomnia night.

Venice was amazing. The shops around Venice had an abundant supply of Hitler figurines and Nazi flags which I found odd and offensive. Besides the septic trash strewn rivers the rest was breathtaking, amazing architecture, you know, go.

We all separated in Venice, I went with Joachim and the Swedes, and Craig and Eric went off on a date it seemed. Steve went off with others. We all took many pictures and drank at little cafes, marveled at gondolas passing by. It was a nice day. I remember the Swedes would get up very early and go to museums and appreciate culture, them being probably 5-10 IQ points higher than us, and not traumatized people, they were smart. We, on the other hand, had to remain high on something and we acted like children, dysfunctional children, the ones that parents protect their children from. We'd smoke hash off of beer cans and shit... I think we corrupted the Swedes, we violated their beliefs, I am guessing they were shocked by our self-loathing ways and the disrespect we exuded wherever we went. We were white trash.

That night we had time off in at the State fair atmosphere in Venice after an intense show, it was like a village gathering or something. Traditional local pride-filled songs were sung with accordion accompaniment, men and women in some sort of traditional garb, then us. It was an awkward juxtaposition to say the least, but everyone, every last grandma enjoyed it a lot, they thought, "this is *the youth*," but it so wasn't. Under park lights in a community field we had a really fun, drunken soccer game with the guys from Kid Commando, we ran and ran, it was a great night. It was so great, being young and healthy and free!

Staying in Genoa, Italy, oh the warm hospitality there... immediately the men took us out on a porch of sorts, demonstrating their prowess and masculinity by rolling their own pasta; the women stayed inside piling on the table all sorts of delicious bread, olives and shit that tasted so fucking good but I will never know exactly what it was. We dined together, broke the bread, had a huge meal. One of the ladies told us that the gent whose house it was, that the guy's father just died days before. Even though we were cretins we managed to be respectful and talk to the dude. We ended up walking through the town of Genoa all night until the morn, we watched the sun come up, embracing each other. We made good friends. I miss these people with all my heart, out there wherever you are, I love you.

Careening across Europe, we stopped on this vast hill, rolling levels, scrub brush looking trees, like something out of *The Godfather II*. This one bathroom we came across had an elevator style door. It looked like a yellow mushroom from WWII. You went in and there was just a hole in the floor but the door shut you in like an elevator, it had a rubber seal, inside, the worst smell ever. I left hoping I never was eaten by something and shit out, especially not by a caravan full of Asian tourists.

We came into Rome on the major motor artery into the city. These motherfuckers on mopeds of all sorts zipped by us and around us on all sides. We took some exit. Marie was the only one confident enough to ask for directions, namely because she was sick of our internal bitching and just wanted to get the fuck out of the van with us. She pulled up next to this random guy and asked how to get to the venue. It turned out this guy was an Elvis impersonator who claimed he had played at the club before. In hindsight, once we got there, it seemed he tried to bogart our credibility to get himself a gig there, and he was definitely a street urchin type. But it was great, Elvis giving us directions.

Once we finally arrived, Rome was hot! A model, an authentic model that is in fashion magazines, came right up to the stage as we started to play. She unzipped these red thigh-high suede boots she had on and erotically took them off, she was far more entertaining to us, I could barely play whilst witnessing this lust-laden performance ongoing before us. Once her boots were off, erotically, she proceeded to head bang and enjoy our quirky worm set. It was great, just great.

They took us to this place during the day to drop our shit off, our sleeping bags and backpacks were all we had besides our musical gear. It was some fort or government barracks or some shit now occupied by squatters, typical of Europe. There are laws or allowances where if you are a landlord and you work away from your property, tenants (read: anarchists) could stay, and if they upkeep or improve your deadbeat shithole, then they become partial or full owners after many years of occupancy, so dumb. This place was something like that, all excited they babbled on about the strengths of the door, the gate, boasted about assaulting police and the cops being defenseless, on and on. At this point, after sitting in France on the military highway for hours and hours in some truck driver union strike situation, I could give a fuck about the anarchist bullshit. I recall wishing some force, a swat team or something, would just sweep in and pummel these wasteoids. But I was mad, I was insane. My father, during the Vietnam War era, was a military cop assigned to the Brown University area to quell the sit-ins and direct actions taken by anti-war students. It was reported within the family that he mercilessly cracked skulls, lowered IQ's, five points a whack, day in, day out. I had fascist blood without even knowing it. Don't get me wrong, I was redder than Red at this time of my life, but even Rosa Luxemburg needed a fucking nap, food, and some sex, I'd imagine.

Once we were inside we wound through a staircase up to a loft area. On one of the landings there was a glassed-in case with a massive cannabis plant inside, very well-presented and pretty to see. The show was a typical crust show in Europe, they pogo and hug each other, writhing in whatever drug concoction they were on, no one had a brain, us included. Of course, we ate the pasta with the runny sauce, again...

We probably got done at 3 am or so. They escorted us back to the squat, the band, Marie, and Cee Cee. It was a scene out of *Dr. Zhivago*, huge open loft with about 30+ mattresses on the floor and about 60 punks in various states of undress, snuggling, fucking, injecting heroin, sleeping. The lights were very low. They had some illegal Gerry-rigged wood stove in the middle of the room and it smelled like smoke, shit, and filth. It disproved all their political arguments through mere observation. Some people didn't read the manuals before blowing their freedom engines. I was most high so I staggered in last, unaware of the greedy, silent game of musical chairs that had happened before me. Everyone had a bed but me (a shitty mattress). I got upset, in the exhausted baby tantrum way, just too tired of it all. The Italian minding the stove and shooting heroin said "no worries," he just went up the anarchist older guy on a mattress near the stove and dragged him off of it, yelled some shit in Italian, pointed a lot. That dude angrily left. I didn't even give a fuck, I just flopped down right there, enjoying his body heat still in the bed. Bugs crawled on me all night, but I was used to this life, you just get up, pick the toenails and burnt matches, cigarette butts, a used bloody band aide, Cheerios, whatever, off the side of your face and start the day. Embrace the "couch scum goalie" identity.

In the morning groans and sniffles awoke us. Hungover people, some dope-sick, chattered in Italian in the corner. This was a real fuckin' skid row situation. Cee Cee had apparently decided (or broke down) in the night, perhaps she just snapped, but she gave herself over to being a "woman of the night." She just walked around in nothing but a thong, her pearly white ass showing to all these male degenerates. No one was shocked but me, I mean, she presented herself so highbrow and intelligent back in Sweden, but now anyone could have her, she stopped caring, she was a prostitute now.

I forgot to mention that Roman was our road manager and was traveling with us at this time. He'd been low key up to this point, but it dawned on me how hard it must have been for this guy because the Midwest was different, industrial, chemical, drunk, and free. Perhaps we were just hanging out with too many weird Polish guys. I think the people in Europe annoyed him at times; sometimes after a long day you just want to go to a comfortable bar or go home and relax. When we were there we were total imbecilic man-children, not acting that way or excited (at first I think the Europeans thought that was what was up), but really lowbrow, and Roman was too. We always had to be "on," or try to be, like, "Oh G_d, they brought the tourists." We were tourists in life. There are times, I must admit, where listening to some Arnold Schwarzenegger motherfucker tell you a monotonous two-hour long story about how intense his band is gets fucking annoying as fuck, like a robot lecture. I could see why Roman was pissed.

Crossing Basque country was interesting, we hung out with some real righteous people, they had two things they thought we thought were interesting, one was Manu Chao and the other was their "uncles" in ETA. We absorbed it all. Up all night talking about some stupid form of Art, Revolution and other radical politics. I always had one foot out the door on this type of stuff, I had been in the South of the USA and I love Loretta Lynn and Conway Twitty; I am not sure these people could ever understand or appreciate that.

Arnau, a good friend, this guy was a cool motherfucker. We went to the club where Joachim was DJing that night, a metal door, we found the address somehow, and this slot opened up with eyeballs peering out. We showed our invitations and were admitted. This was really intense. Everyone was cool in there, it was a modern place, and we must have seemed like fucking street thugs to these folks at first. I drank too much, took their pristine skateboard out all night and thrashed the shit out of it, ollied over a homeless guy on a mattress successfully that night, they thought I was Tony Hawk's dysfunctional brother or something, Vinny Hawk? Very, very drunk. It was a very chic and hip place. I woke up and miraculously my brain still somehow worked, it was at that level of partying.

Arnau took us to a great restaurant off of La Rambla, he was adamant about being a Catalan as opposed to Spanish. The restaurant owner greeted us, he was from Serbia and the food he cooked was this amazingly well done comfort food, little pies of chicken and veggies. It was the best damn meal. The following day we walked to Sagrada Familia and ate some tapas on the way, this particular one was a piece of bread with a cherry tomato smeared on top, I still don't recall what they call this, some bruschetta type stuff, but it was awesome. It was so pleasant seeing the art school students drinking beers at 11 AM, just tiny beers less than ½ a pint, it was proper, it was part of this culture. Sagrada Familia was all it was cracked up to be, majestic, intense, I was such an architecture naive, Arnau lovingly schooled our uneducated minds like a guide, we learned so much in our travels. What an erection! Mazes of beauty, I won't spoil the glory of this place for you but Christ, please put it on your list of things to do before you turn cold and die. It is worth it. Back in Barcelona, we played an okay show, but Europe had moved into a hybrid of Rock and Electronic Dance Music, Arnau and Joachim were interested in DJ'ing. Late at night they played this secret "members only" club. The graffiti in this town was amazing; I usually don't like this form of "art," but this was irresistible, it fit the environment rather than being some dog piss on a fire hydrant shit we see back home. Everyone was benefitting and so many great bands were brought in. I am not sure, but I like to believe this was trail-blazing also. I mean, bands had toured here before but at this time in the late 1990's this was unique, the music being presented on a weekly basis in this area was real and I hope people got something out of it all.

The process of contributing to this scene was the most fun time of everything we ever did and probably our greatest achievement. So sad to see it go. We flew back home, so, so depressed, it is so sad to end an important mission, you wonder if you will ever be able to do it again, on the road again right Willy, well, we'd hope so, always.

3 days in Amsterdam...

September

 tue 12 holland tba
 wed 13 belgium tba
 thu 14 belgium tba
  fri 15 france rennes le jardin moderne
 sat 16 france tba
 sun 17 france poitiers confort moderne
 mon 18 france paris les istants chavires
 tue 19 france lyon kaminstubchen
 wed 20 germany munich club zwei
 thu 21 austria tba
 fri 22 slovenia ilirska bistrica MKNZ
 sat 23 croatia zagreb KSET
 sun 24 off in wien
 mon 25 austria vienna chelsea
 tue 26 italia trento angi
 wed 27 italia tba
 thu 28 italia roma tba
 fri 29 italia milano cox 18
 sat 30 germany bielefeld AJZ
 october>sun 1 germany stuttgart tbc
 mon 2 germany dresden eastclub bischofswerda
 tue 3 denmark copenhagen loppen tbc
 wed 4 sweden malmo smalands
 thu 5 denmark aalborg 1000 fryd tbc
 fri 6 germany tba
 sat 7 holland conspiracy antwerp tba

Some odd jobs came up in the interim, we played this really fucking odd show in Boston; it was in Chinatown, the show was with US Maple. Hibarger's band opened. It was an elite gathering, we played and those silly guys in US Maple just still didn't want to talk to us. Spring came and we were invited to play MIT, Noam Chomsky's place of employment, he shat there on a lunch break or two which made us happy, just knowing that, but that is as close as we got, that thought... Playing at MIT was fun honestly, we played with Wesley Willis and the MIT Gay Men's Choir. They had this pig roast going on, at the time I was veg so I didn't indulge, there was this carcass on a spit out in the quad, we played as a foredrop for this, it was hostile. After we played to an uneventful crowd who cared more about their Bob Marley flags hanging out of their windows of the dorms. But redemption time certainly came, major chronic used. Students kept offering more money; all we wanted was food. "You guys are really into what you do, aren't you?" Biggest insult. Playing for people with no emotions. Whatever, we got pot in that kid's dorm, best pot I've ever smoked, MIT shit we called it as in, "gimmee some more of that 'MIT shit'," in the van. We loved that THC MIT shit.

We went across this damn country again. There was a big club in San Francisco, Bottom Of The Hill; this was where I met Meg Watjen, a good friend. She was a very spunky person and a great booking agent. She worked for Sub Pop and we were all enamored with that, although honestly at the time we were just another band that I don't think she gave two shits about. All I can remember is thinking that she seemed completely consumed by this dramatic American Psycho boyfriend.

He was a real piece of shit. We were at an after-party once and he threw a drink in a girl's face. I remember me and Gabe from The Locust wanting to kick the fucking shit out of that guy, but like a typical pussy he ran out of the building. You can call it "white knighting," but shit like that made my blood boil, and I don't care what anyone thinks, I'm not going to allow that around anywhere that I am hanging out. It is sad how out of a line up of one thousand guys, certain women can pick out, with complete accuracy, which ones are the batterer types; it is like clockwork, they pick out the abusers... Some women just repeat this relationship pattern over and over.

Nevertheless, it was a great venue and we had a pretty decent show there. We played some other half-decent shows there, including one with The Locust and Blood Brothers back in the day, which was a big success. To be completely honest with you, our sole focus was on playing our show, and then jutting across the street as fast as humanly possible to the Lusty Lady. There was some kind of progressive bullshit policy there were the dancers had a cooperative and were paid fairly; it was basically a huge circle and guys would go into isolated peep booths, you'd pay into a slot and then the window would open and you could look into whoever was dancing at the time. Some of us got individual lap dances which were in private rooms. I never did, but it looked fun. We frequented this establishment so often we got to know many of the ladies there, who ironically, 9 out of 10 times prior to the shift, were at our shows. They were our same age and some were fans. We mutually respected one another's performances but for very different reasons. It was a great place. I do recall our tour manager Rob being nauseated because, not only could you see the woman erotically performing, you could look across the circle without any problem and see what other men were doing in their stalls. I had no shame jaggin' off. It was absolutely a blue balls high pressure stressful situation; it had to be released, I had to beat the bishop. But apparently he had witnessed from across the octagon, my fervor, it affected his ability to maintain an erection. I probably still owe the guy 5 bucks for that cold shower situation, sorry Rob. There was a poor bastard who worked there late at night who was a fan, his job was to mop up the stalls after all of us sweat hogs dumped our baby batter on the floor. I recall seeing his utility closet where he kept the mop, and on the mop bucket itself, one of those yellow industrial things, there was and probably still is an Arab on Radar *Soak The Saddle* 4x4 sticker. We thought that was the best thing ever. It really summed up what we were all about musically.

We would always be playing new material, people would be anticipating the last record, the one we just put out, but the lag time was so long we'd already moved on to the next one, so it was bittersweet for some folks. We would always go over the set list prior to the show. We'd throw in old and new (unheard) songs to keep it interesting. We'd show up in uniform. On some tours we would only wear our uniforms offstage and on, no other clothes. We would set up all the amps, guitars turned up, and leave the stage, lights off. Then I'd insist we all "did the eyes" meaning looked each other in the eyes. Sometimes the guys bitched and poo poo'ed this ritual but it was important, it meant "where you at" and at times know one knew, even he didn't, where he was at. We'd take the stage quick, the industrial lights would go on and we'd hit it, usually real hard, with a solid song #1, #3, Birth Control Blues... Then the shit either went off or it didn't. I appreciated the times most when it didn't because that meant WAR. And we would fight to shock, engage, or physically intimidate whoever was there. We got a reaction either good or bad. The ritual was going to happen.

Somewhere in San Francisco we landed. We never had the pleasure of playing this venue but we always ended up going to this bar The Eagle, an old guard hangout. I remember being enamored with framed bloody tighty whitey underwear the local guys commemorated the rapings of young boys, the "old guard" of San Fran, these sick degenerative pedophiles. Hollywood types would frequent this place and the community supported it all, but who am I to judge?

Down when we were in San Diego we would travel out to play the Che Café which was the student club on the campus of UCSD. All I can remember is a small lodge sort of venue, it had rafters, there were tons of flyers on bulletin boards everywhere for all sorts of causes, "Free Mumia" and "Give Lollipops to Street Sex Workers," all this shit which was taken so seriously. One fascinating aspect of this venue was the woods up in back of it. It accentuated the very different climate than we were accustomed to back home. There were groves of jade plants and rubber tree plants everywhere. I recall a blown out greenhouse out back there where we smoked some doobage and I made out with a girl. These little moments meant so much back then, yet more evidence and data that went into reasons we should keep going on, you decide...

At the time Joey from The Locust was finishing art school. I think we staying up all night in his fucked up trailer that the school allowed to be on campus for some communist reason. I sat with the poor bastard while he rushed to finish all sorts of shit; we were a burden, but maybe it was good to have some company in the midst of all that shit that seemed so important at the time and really wasn't; who knows?

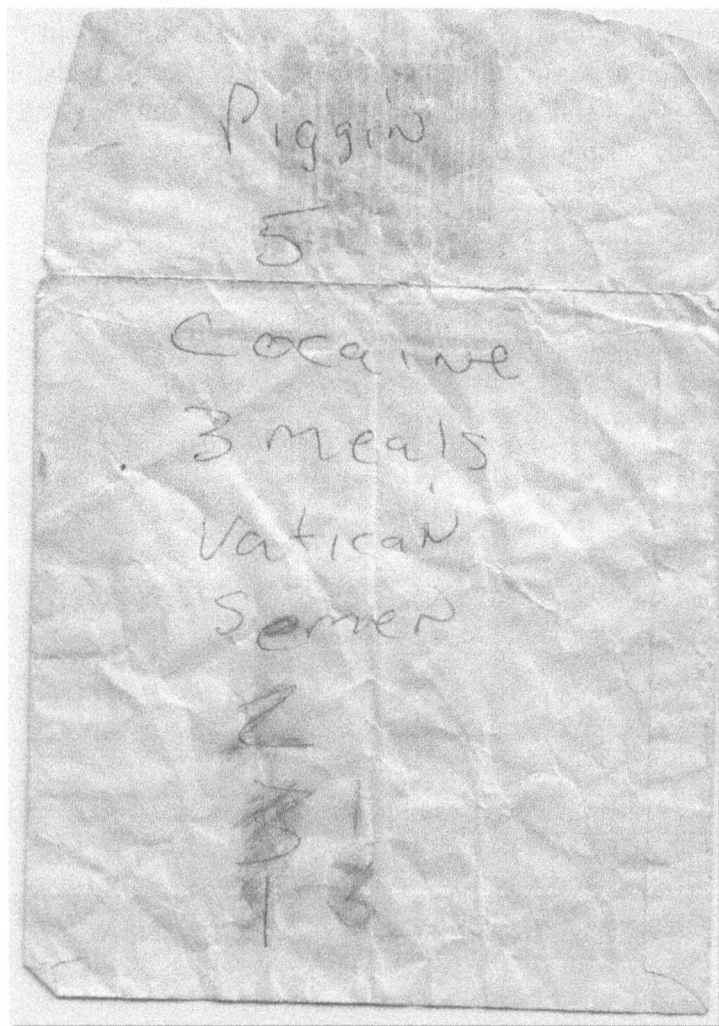

Piggin

5

Cocaine

3 meals

Vatican

Server

2
3
1

The Oops Tour, Christ, we called and called Fort Thunder looking for a commitment from Lightning Bolt to do the tour over and over and over. It was frustrating as shit. Somehow it was our job to be chasing Chippendale down Broadway to confirm that they were on board. We found that little Peter Pan riding his BMX bike across town. All four of us in a car, lurking around corners, we made him an offer he couldn't refuse, you know, accommodations, money, booking it all, that sort of shit. He used to steal from Whole Foods bulk bins, carob was his favorite item. What he would do was get a bag and fill it one inch with flour, and then he'd take another bag and put about two pounds of carob balls in it, then he would take yet a third bag and put more flour in that bag, somehow he disguised his carob and got a greater bulk rate for his snacking pleasure. He seemed to always get what he wanted and in this case it was carob. I am not sure why I always make this association, but he was very much like Sting, same attitude, whatever that is, tantric lifestyle, perhaps Scientology, raw ego… But the guy played some sick drumming.

This was foundation of the so-called rivalry between Hella and Lightning Bolt: Hella and Lightning Bolt shared the same genetic imprint, the virtuoso drummer DNA molecule, the mutations started mostly as shit-talk and rumors from the audience about who was better at bombastic drumming, Zach Hill or Chippendale, which we never took seriously at all, we appreciated both of their music and saw them as separate species all together. The audience did not. This all came to a controlled experiment in fission on the Oops Tour, I think in California. Hella was nearing the finish of their set on stage, LB was set up on the floor.

Lightning Bolt tried to jump off the end of the last note of their last song, their whole thing that they used to do to people, which we never let them do to us, not even once, even though they tried, we used to psych them out and play another song right over them when they tried that bullshit, we were louder than them because we were playing through the PA which worked in our favor for once. But what happened here in California was that Hella kept playing and Lightning Bolt started playing and tempos and temperatures were rising, then Gibson stopped playing bass, and five more minutes in Spencer stopped playing guitar. Just the two were left now, in fact I think Gibson just left the place all together. And this is where the fucking drum stampede began, sometimes they were in sync but mostly it was cacophony, just raw and barbaric testosterone aggression. Hundreds witnessed in awe as the two alpha males fought for the right to leave their genetic imprint. Whose canine teeth were larger? Glands swollen, hands bloody, blue photons shimmered off of their butt tissue inflamed in all their glory, blazing, they drummed on and on with dust rising up off of the floor of this venue. This went on for about forty-five minutes until someone (I won't reveal who) keeled over in defeat. Human Biology will never be the same after this day.

To add insult to injury, and perhaps to maintain a dominance hierarchy, when Hella came to Providence, they were playing at Monnahasset Mills. While Hella was playing inside, for a minute Steve and I were outside bullshitting while quite surprisingly Lightning Bolt started to set up in the parking lot of the venue. It was the dead of winter and we weren't really sure why they were doing this, but it all makes biological sense now. They blasted over Hella's set for a good solid five seconds, then the mechanical world took over and some sort of pin sheered loose from Chippendale's kick pedal, something essential to its mechanics. The pin bounced across the parking lot and into some unknown culvert never to be seen again. At that point Chippendale just snapped, after futzing around with it for a minute or two, everyone in the club had come out to see what that racket was all about outside that only lasted 5 seconds but was really loud. He became irate and started going up to people asking them for a drum pedal to borrow. By the time he got to me I was really high, and he was screaming frantically about something, "Do you have a nail? Anything?" I just shook my head no. I'm not exactly sure how this reproductive battle ended this time but both guys are great drummers regardless of their baboon-like behaviors.

Once Brian Peterson and Ben McOsker solidified all the dates and it seemed all the bands were on board, we got ready to leave, same van, this tour we decided to wear black Dickies as our uniform which looked really badass in a Johnny Cash type of way. We hadn't been talking much to each other a week before, the typical routine was someone would pick up the van and then go door to door picking up the other band members, after we had loaded up the van the night before at the space in Johnston. It was sort of a tradition to look our best, at least at the beginning of tours. Steve was nominated as the first person to get the van, he came to pick me up before Eric and Craig. The night before I had decided to shave my beard into a fu manchu mustache and let my hair grow out naturally which is probably one of the most insane Jew-fros, right up there with Art Garfunkel and Bob Dylan. At the time this look was unheard of, way before it had its revival. So when Steve picked me up he barely recognized me. I looked like a thug from the adult correctional institute. And he just said, "oh my fucking G_d." I put my guitars in the van. We both knew it was going to be an amazing time. We were so excited about the roster of all these shows. Brian Peterson made a detailed tour itinerary and people were coming off and on this tour from various regions of the country, representing the best of the underground scene in each region. People had different tastes. It brought out the elitism of the East Coast and NY attitude and highlighted the laissez-faire musicianship of the West Coast. Everybody had a significant contribution to this organic musical experience. I've said this before but it seemed a lot like *Festival Express*, Janis, The Band, Grateful Dead, and Great Speckled Bird. On the Oops tour roster there were many greats. The first night was out East, The Locust had travelled far and wide to play it. We all felt each other out, it was storming and norming of the group that would travel together. After the first show, we all hung out in the parking lot of the venue, there were people blasting off roman candles, wigs were worn, it was ego central. Everyone was uptight, out-doing one another with jokes about hair-dos and clothes, riffs and beats. This type of thing had never been tried before. It was competitive but in a sweet way. People eventually eased the fuck up, this was our "social" where we met before the seminar of Music began, out there on the road, facing the public. These shows were huge, very well-attended and to the lucky ones they probably saw, in my opinion the best musical happening that had happened in a very long time. I dare to say, that for the type of music I love, this was "Woodstock," the best, the presentation of true passion and the sign of our times. So little has been documented or discussed about the Oops Tour, some experiments were not replicated, the data too far out for people to grasp, such a shame...

There was this guy Mick Barr who played in Orthrelm, he was a guitar virtuoso, I never could quite understand how he got his guitar tone, it was a very processed sound, but he was like dammed Yngwie Malmsteen on the fret board. It was quite a fireworks display. He looked like somebody that could have been in the band Phish, and all the technical geeks idolized his musical prowess. There was a masturbatory aspect to it, but all in all I thought it was something like, shit I'll never be able to do that. I've never devoted myself to anything that much in my whole fuckin' life. He was a priest. There were less pious acts who were centralized more on party/fun, like Rah Brahs. We seriously partied with them. I remember the drummer was wearing a black bra while he played. They were with us in New Orleans; this was a night that blossomed into a heavy-duty party situation in the French Quarter. I remember it being Brian Gibson of Lightning Bolt's birthday and we were in a tranny bar. Once they found out, he ended up making out and dancing while the divas of the club stuffed dollar bills down his homemade trousers. It was a blast.

New Orleans was a great time, we played a great place on Bourbon St. amidst the bar gravy and the street performers, it is always Mardi Gras here, but especially when it is Mardi Gras. Walked around Jackson Square for a while tripping over homeless people and filth. The venue was really cool, it had a great mural inside.

Everyone went separate ways, we had an intimate dinner with Quintron and Ms. Pussycat, they were so kind. I think I ate fried oysters. It was her birthday and they invited us out with them, she is such a kind soul, I remember wishing that they were my brother and sister, how much fun we would have had playing together as kids. It was a special night, that Preservation Hall vibe, I love it in the Big Easy, I'd live in the French Quarter if I could afford to.

Of course, there were awkward moments during the Oops Tour, we were at some house in who the hell knows where. There was a well-established "Fort Thunder look" which consisted of recycled clothing, patches, dirtiness, custom made t-shirts all that art school stuff at the time. Chippendale, Brinkman, and a few others at the Fort consciously, and to this day, maintained a hair-do that was unique, it was cutting your own hair, presumably without a mirror, at least at first, just hacking away, which produced an uneven and chopped up mess, but ultra-cute in the right critical settings, it added art credibility to their mere presence. Well, Jeff Rosenberg of Pink and Brown fame had tagged along on the tour as their "tour manager" or some such role. He went into this blown out house we were crashing at and came out of the bathroom, highly uncharacteristically (he looked like a normal guy but) he had the hair-do, he had carved up his head in like fashion, probably for the tour. This went over like a lead balloon, unfortunately, it was disingenuous and made everyone feel uncomfortable, but hell, I give the guy an A+ for effort. It was the energy of it all, people just wanted to come along, join this circus, and be a part of what was going on, and he wanted to be Brian

Chippendale.

The Get Hustle was a really great bunch of people. Valentine who sang, Mack on organ, Maxamillion who played some sick drums, and Andy, bass. I think they like lived by a certain occult code. Mack and Valentine had been in a relationship, I didn't know what happened, but at some of these shows there was music, but then also this whole non-verbal conversation was going on between them. Who knows about what, but my guess it was deep, rather sexual, possibly BDSM, and it wove in and out of the music. Valentine was so down to earth; I spent many nights talking with her about all sorts of shit, she was strong. They were like fine antiques, in their unique garb and intense personalities, really lovely, cool people. Valentine, I loved her, everyone loved her; she was so beautiful and seductive. I felt sad when this leg of the tour ended and we had to travel on. Whatever their vibe was it felt so good, like a comfy fire on some Berber rug in a monastery in some distant country.

We have that one soft porn video out of all of us in a male hot basement, just being awkward, all in our underwear. And JP is on the washing machine on his laptop. He must have been a very hard man to please. We played like puppy dogs, doing stupid shit like teenagers. It was never more serious than playing fetch, rolling over and occasionally dry-humping each other.

We were hanging out in New Orleans on the Oops tour, I was sitting on a couch and I whipped out a fat joint, Chippendale's girlfriend came over and wanted to smoke. He got a little agitated with her at this prospect, went on a rant about "stoners," I suppose it seemed like I was corrupted and he didn't want her to be corrupted too. I'd never seen someone so irritated. He rescued her from running away with The Grateful Dead. His reaction reminded me of Feyd from *Dune*, same vibe, Sting... He needed to smoke some of that shit, for real. Playing with Lightning Bolt, man, they had a marketing sense, what we called "the RISD Bat Signal," they sent out a message at the 11th hour and hundreds of people would still show up, scarcity, they knew how to harness that shit. I wonder if they teach this at RISD? It reeked of elitist mentality, country clubs ran on this energy, but then again, they were really damn good. Their peak, if I were to say, was around the time of their "Frere Jacques" period, whatever that song was, the one that sounded like that, was just awesome. We, on the other hand, were unwanted stepchildren at the birthday party always. I have to admit we were totally jealous, in case that's not obvious.

ALL ACCESS
★ ★ PASS ★ ★

Name: _OOPS!_

Date: _7/9/02_

Authorized by: _CJS_

FIRST AVENUE & 7th St entry

Chapter 19 – Musician-Assisted Suicide

One grotesque comment I must make about Music is my fear and anger about bands that had it in the pocket at one time and then petered out. I think of the worst culprits, Metallica. Was it the booze? Was it money? Something squashed their music. Soundgarden, many, many others, us included, the music is formed. Songs get good. You listen to your own music and sincerely feel, "this is what I would listen to if I were me," then something happens, kaput. Perhaps it is that the music is discussed ad nauseam, but the method of arriving at it may be too private. Obviously, James Hetfield was the person with the methods, then he felt, fuck it. Do these assholes deserve this? Do they deserve the drinking/drugging/fucking into oblivion to get these songs out? Or do I choose, like, my life over their needs, do I need to die more, one thousand deaths, suffering for what, I'm rich? For us it was more a matter of exploitation and putting the brakes on certain members, taking your own path and dancing with your own corpse. The guys back home used to say, "they were trying to put me in a dress." Some don't let that happen, then the staggering afterwards is *The Black Album*, the let down shit, the method of greatness is not followed. Once you fall out of love I'm not sure you can ever get back, what you have is some bastardized version of something great. Captain Beefheart, Black Flag, they all knew this. The new girlfriend sucks compared to Camelot. If you hear something that is spot-on enjoy it before the divorce comes, before the chain pulls, before the method is forgotten or purposefully hidden from everyone. There is only one good cure for this sickness, making the next one better than the last, better methods dethroning those of the last, if you can't do that you do not know and as Wittgenstein advised one must then pass over in silence. I respect every artist who just quit rather than not recognizing this fact. All this: Jane's Addiction, The Cure, crying to Joy Division songs played over and over… I wasn't in love, but I related to loving feelings, I never looked at the red flags and flaws of who was supposedly giving the love. It was a horrid struggle for self-worth, self-love. Fucking Hell!

Late in our days, we went to LA to play a label showcase, this was at the urging of Brian Peterson who so badly wanted us to get a break. I feel bad, it was obvious to us we were dead in the eyes of the mainstream, but he was such a believer, he had faith in a better world where we would be something to listen to, but we knew, especially at this time, we were just another misfit organization, reserved for the fringe, the high IQ fringe of weirdos who could find us. The guy from the block would not side with us, he couldn't, more boring acts blocked the way. The showcase consisted of a bunch of bands, up like strippers we went, pole-dancing with Fishbone, that cracked out dude Anthony? He was up in our faces. He seemed desperate. He was handing out flyers for his showcase a few days later, begging, he had some affiliation with the club (Knitting Factory in LA). Some guy claiming to be Pete Towshend's boyfriend came up to me and said, "Pete would love to hear you," and me believing him and giving him a free record. I willingly became a sucker; embarrassing how I tasted LA's dark side, the sucking for coke side, Less Than Zero. There were many times we were humiliated like this, playing with Melt Banana, them staying with Eric, the guitarist leaving bloody band aids in his bathtub, these people were used to having maids. We were their maids apparently, so rude.

Late days, the End Times, the shows with Milemarker (at the request and set up of Brian P.) Eric writing his poetry book, and Al Burian from MileMarker calling him out for selling rape fantasy books at under-age shows to children. Eric's face grew pale and a gross, green look came across it, he offered little defense, he just slithered away. I was rip shit mad, I argued with him like – look, just defend your Art! Henry Miller did! It is satire and designed to provoke! I pleaded with him to use the NWA, gangster rap argument, this is where I'm from, my reality, I can say whatever I need to describe my reality. He cowardly said very little other than he will continue to sell his book at our merchandise table. This was probably the spark that led to the fire of our break-up as a band. A leopard does not change its spots, ever...

It was a hard emotion to endure, I can only describe it as falling for manipulation, then realizing it, and the perpetrator realizing you realize it, then coexisting in that state for many years. My honeymoon ended quickly, what could we do? Play music, that is all. Come together over interesting things: art, people, food. But there was little love there, always mistrust, one foot out the door, many hurtful, unresolved events. We were always curiously unresolved, needing each other's strengths to succeed but able to live without it all.

We only played at the Dirt Palace in Providence once to my recollection, ironically, and it was while touring with Milemarker, booked by Brian at Skin Graft (both bands' tour). We opened. I feel bad because within the margins they set on things, we must have instigated a lot of problems. It was almost like we forced people to vouch for our PC safeness and no one really did, and we were not safe at this time in my estimation. But we played, and everyone had a great time. All I can say about the Dirt Palace is that it was a place of healing. I'd go to their dance parties if invited. They would pair men with men and women with women regardless of heterosexuality. I'd go to shows. I was working at The Living Room learning sound and the Dirt Palace had a small mixer, I'd just go over there to look at it and talk about decibels and shit with Zoe; I had a bad feeling, perhaps paranoid, but some people were staring and some thought I was mansplaining shit or something. I was scared, I wasn't comfortable with myself and I cannot understand all the theories and gaze and all that. I remember they had this large, ceiling-high display made out of cardboard, it was built into a wall sort of where two or three people could go in the big cardboard box. It was a huge computer that said, "ask any question," almost like Lothar or Hal. I pushed the button, some milk bottle cap thing, and it spit out a blank piece of receipt paper. I was so severely depressed, had just come off a long tour, tired, hadn't slept. I wrote "Why me?" and put it back. It answered, "Because you are a great person." On that night, that message probably saved my life. I felt like someone cared; every night these shows felt like no one did, that was the message they were delivering over and over. This just struck me as such an unconditional gesture. It's sick and for all the wrong reasons, I tried to get closer to Zoe. Someone, maybe Steve, told me it was her who wrote it; fucking bros guys are, it really is true. But I innocently just wanted to find a way to feel again. So selfish. It didn't work out, she had just ended a relationship, I was insane. She was struggling harder than I was and her hard work paid off. I just embarrassed myself and moved on.

None of this shit really matters or makes sense unless you are listening to the music. If you are, and it still doesn't make sense, fine but, just remember, there isn't much else left, if you are working back from the line we drew in the sand. Whatever music you like, your Cyndi Lauper or whatnot, I just want to point out that we knew every last note to our songs, perfected the songs as what they were, every motive for every note was analyzed with meticulous detail. The whole concept, we understood it, wrote it and threw it aside. There really is nothing left but us and if you settle for less or can't do better, don't be proud, it just means we are fucked and seeking comfort in that is agreeing with defeat, death and the end of human existence. We may not have been perfect, but to give a lead a platform like that, such power, G_d, how could you not feel like you owed me/us something, pushing through the riffs, the builds. You will never have an opportunity like that again and you blew it; what a waste.

Things were really looking up while we were going down. We had a full 4-page article written about us in *Thrasher Magazine*, this was a personal high for me growing up being a skate-rat and all. We had arrived, but were asked to leave shortly after we got there.

This book has no readers so beware, shit got intense, and we were trying so hard to find an "in," we were offered a spot on the next Van's Warped Tour.

Kevin from The Living Room was our sound guy for some of these gigs, I mean, we begged him to come along, he had taken the time and talked to us and actually understood our dual speaker rigs, he mixed us well at the club in the past, we had some delusion of supporting a whole road crew with us some day, you know, when we were as big as The Pixies, the reality was that we ended up taking oxycontin on the way to Purchase College on a weekend trip. We could barely make sense of the show and he could barely mix our sound. It was absurd, but it got better. The gig was playing with The Locust, Biz Markie and Gwar. Gwar set up for three days, sent their road crew to set up all this gory shit; then decided to not come, and they didn't play. It was pure bureaucratic waste, like the DMV only worse. Biz Markie showed up and didn't talk to anyone. Of course we had "green room" access because we were a "talent" booked to "perform" this "event." We walked backstage to see him entertaining his entourage and eating a big ass bucket of Kentucky Fried Chicken. It was an amazing night; he scratched the turntable using the blubber under his chin, it was perfect. We played *Yahweh* to the brightest minds in their most relaxed moments and all they wanted was fun, not to think, fun. We dumped out our hearts, but this was not our venue, there was no suffering here, nothing we could latch on to, no one to scare, no one to relate to, we just played and that was that. They tried to use the light show to enhance our lecture in Music, but to no avail, we played stark, nude in our honesty to no one who could care and why blame them, we were unimportant at this moment and it was best we moved on. We realized no one knew us, not our label, manager, promoters, no one and we simply couldn't entertain... we might as well have been playing our kazoos or brought up some male slaves for beatings by their dominatrix, this had nothing to do with us. It was a mistake.

We played our last show at North 6 in Brooklyn. It was good. We didn't know it would be the end but it was. We ended in full bloom, at the height of it, playing our best music. I was satisfied with this; it was a perfect end to a perfect thing, bookends, and closure...

Through all this cynical irony, we arrived, now we always knew exactly what we were doing with our music, we knew how to get out what we came up with, how to play it, it was an affirmation of our own creation every time we played, every show had a happy ending. As short as our sets were, we maintained a reason to stay alive as a band, namely, for our audiences to see the next shows in a year or 6 months, whenever we could come back to visit. Sweating under the lights, we gave it everything we had, every night. Many people, loving people, supported us to do this. The feeling was that this mission had been accomplished. Satisfaction, at least in my mind, had set in, the edge was duller, but still sharp enough, the beats got slower. Our eventual break-up broke so many hearts, our own being the least of them.

Exclusive: Arab On Radar's first interview since re-forming
BY SEAN CARNAGE JUNE 7, 2010

"Everyone should experience Arab On Radar at least once in their life." – Arab On Radar

Underground music icons Arab On Radar are back with their first tour (and new music) since 2002. This is really exciting, because with the exception of The Flying Luttenbachers and XBXRX (and U.S. Maple with whom AOR share a certain "precisely wrong" musical aesthetic), they were the only band to get me through the dark 'n sad (though immaculately coiffed) era of the late 1990s and early 2000s when emo was dominating seemingly everywhere from punk squat to outdoor arena. AAAARGH...Thank goodness that's over.

Now all the AOR players—Mr. OCD, Mr. Pottymouth, Mr. Clinical Depression, Mr. Type A—have returned to save our insanity once again. Each is represented in this SEANCARNAGE.COM exclusive interview.

Arab On Radar were one of those rare groups to rise out of the muck of '90s post-Grunge with a unique sound and presentation. They were equal parts simian punk rock (complete with demented ass-touching and other monkey-like rituals) and cutting-edge psychedelia (the band mapped out a new synaethesial frontier that Frank Zappa or Faust would no doubt have been eager to explore).

Arab On Radar were super nice, insightful guys, too. I thought they'd be little messes in real life (with their insane live show it was only natural to think that). But when AOR slept on my floor a few times back in Cleveland, they were ever so neat and tidy.

So when this legendary group announced they were getting back together a few months back, I immediately sent interview questions. Today, Arab On Radar were gracious enough to respond:

Just to make sure I've got all the details right, what personnel are currently Arab on Radar? And are you still based out of Providence?

Mr. OCD – Drummer
Mr. Pottymouth – Singer
Mr. Clinical Depression – Guitar
Mr. Type A – Guitar
Weasel Walter – Producer
Sonny Kay – Manager
Jasmine Hughes – Tour Manager
Bobby Missile – Booking Agent (USA)
Vincent Royers – Booking Agent (Europe)

We are from Providence, RI not a thing has changed about that.

How would you describe your current musical aesthetic?
Arab On Radar

When did you start thinking/talking about this new tour?
March 2010.

What's the sartorial concept for the upcoming shows?
The concept is Blue uniforms this time. Also, we are trying to give away one unique item at every show as to make it a special occasion. Limited to about 200 per night.

What about the music?
Setlists are based on what songs flow best musically from one to another. It sometimes takes us a few shows to understand which songs to put where, but it usually depends on how we feel about an hour before the show. If it is going to be a psychedelic night then its one way, if people seem to want to go nuts with us, then it will be our more intense songs. The setlist depends on how we feel on the ground when we arrive at a location.

What turns you on most about making music with the other guys in the band?
We have been developing Arab On Radar for many years.

How have you guys stayed in touch?

No, we did not stay in touch. We still like all the music we always have and that is too much to list here. As we have said elsewhere, we listen to our own music and derive influence from our own music, this is how we proceed. We encourage other musicians to use this method it is the key to creating new and original music.

How do you prepare physically for a new tour? Obviously you guys expend a ton of effort when you play. Do you ever feel like: my body can't take any more of this?
Not really, we are always ready to play and perform, and once we get into the state of mind required to do our show there is little consideration for the abuse our bodies take. The next morning is another story.

What's happening in music right now that most excites you?
Whartscape 2010 in Baltimore is a prime example of many amazing musicians, who have developed some amazing things, performing together. The influence such events have on culture is impressive.

Arab On Radar has always had a mongoloid/scatological/disturbingly satirical edge. That's taboo for a lot of folks. How and when did you, as performers, discover that you could relate uncomfortable concepts to an audience as a team?

Perhaps the parts of our music that are scatological just are the most salient. There is a lot of deep stuff in our music. The parts that may be taboo we decided to do because it is reality and we are not joking with our music. It is music that reflects reality in this day and age. Many people are stuck in the past, but we dwell in the present. We are mindful.

Often it is not just us playing, many of the people who go into it with us are just as responsible for making it happen as we are. It is a ritual for the people who go into the music.

What songs should fans expect to hear—and perhaps not hear—in your current set list?
They can expect to hear about 5 of our old songs from Soak the Saddle and Yahweh or the Highway, and probably only three of the brand new songs we have written. They won't hear all of our new songs at one show, we will mix that up from show to show so that we have some room to play some old ones.

The musical landscape—labels, magazines, etc—has been literally turned upside down in the past 15 years. How are you going to do things differently now to make a connection with new fans?

We are making an album. We are writing and recording. We are not on any label at this point but we are talking with some. We hope to get our music out to as many people as we can. As much as it seems like things are upside down, for us this is not really the case, our people have always sought us out and have come to see us because it is what it is and they are a part of that. Without the people on our side there would be no us. We perform in a way that is very extreme and we try our best to get our music out on record (because we are vinyl fans ourselves) and we always try to have amazing art with all of our releases. We also have arabonradar.info to keep people connected with our work. The normal "social networking" sites have some additional information about us every so often, but we do not maintain it personally.

Why do you think that your music is so compelling for so many after all these years?
What makes us compelling is that we try to play our own style of music and people enjoy our live show very much, not to sound like fuckfaces but, it is unlike anything else ever done. Everyone should experience Arab On Radar at least once in their life.

Have you seen that SNL skit where the dudes (Fred Armsen & Dave Grohl among others) "get the old band back together" at the wedding reception?
We have seen it, yes.

If you could reunite a band from back in the day— perhaps one that you'd even want to tour with—who would it be and why?

The Cars.

Lady Gaga or Ke$ha? Explain.
Cher because we want to go where Sonny Bono has gone.

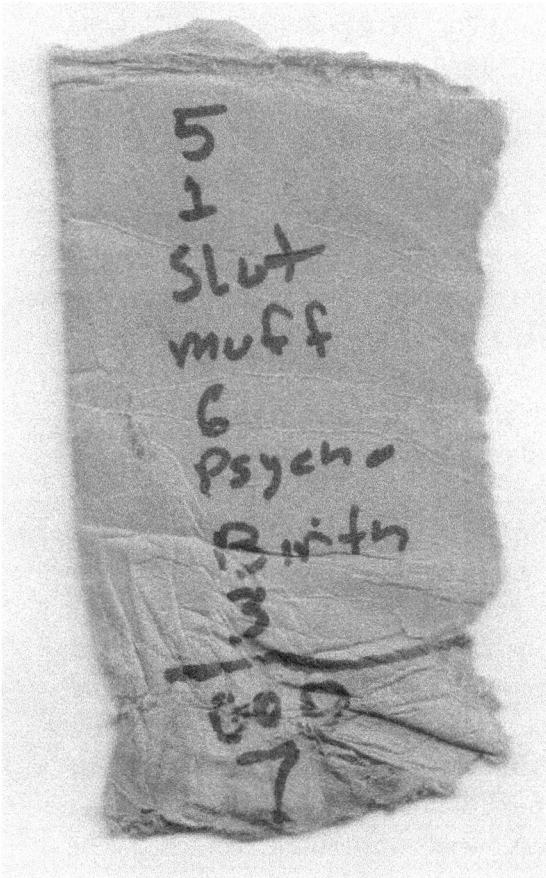

Chapter 20 – Midnight Relapse

I still hung out on the scene. I'd go to shows as much as I could, I was in college; I joined the International Socialists Organization. What did you do that for? I was real passionate about human rights, equality, and justice. Went to protest the war in 2003 with Joan Baez, that was fun, then I came back driven and on to the next mission. I was reading Ward Churchill and Bill Ayers deeply at the time. Word got out that a Nazi protest was going to take place somewhere in Boston on Martin Luther King Jr. Day. We found out they were going to show up at Roxbury's Twelfth Baptist Church to demonstrate. I felt like I couldn't get the word out fast enough. I called friends and Bob Otis and Kaleigh were two friends who responded. We drove up there that day. I remember taking the T once we got up there and we left our knives in my car. Even though we could have been harmed it was not right to bring those with us. Upon arrival, the scene was positive, numbers-wise, there were anarchists, socialists, Stalinists, and clergy. Some ISO guy asked us to keep the crowd moving, show a strong force, he suggested we walk in a circle, showing devotion, in front of the church in the street. Around we went and I started to feel bad asking Bob and K to do this, it was apparent that no one was going to come today. We went on a wild goose chase, over hill, over dale to chase after Nazis at various T stops, running down the Boston Common at one point, it dawned on me that this was a wild goose chase. We left talking about "what-if scenarios" and how mad we were that this is what it takes to live normally and in peace these days. I soured with the ISO due to the message I got when we all met again. It was something along the lines of, Tracy, in Chicago, felt that our chapter in Providence should switch direction and stop doing Anti-War activities, shifting total focus on to immigration issues. I am all for both causes, but the way people just mindlessly gave up on so much work and followed orders creeped me the fuck out. I quit, but it is like the concept of G_d, there is organized religion, directing, and then there is your own relationship with the mighty unknown, no one should interfere with that.

We tried to keep busy and decided to make the Arab On Radar movie that I titled, "Sunshine for Shady People." It was a compilation of footage that Craig had filmed over the years of the band, many shows, some funny interviews etc. He was a mess and so was the footage; my wife was hired to edit it into a cohesive documentary, and somehow it got cobbled together with a lot of editing out of people's bad ideas. I think it is a pretty neat document for what she had to work with. It seems to have dropped into obscurity, even though 31G, our label at the time put it out, it seems to have been purposely buried in the closet of time. When it came out we got mixed reviews; here is a positive one which reveals where we were mentally at this point. It was written by the great musical writer Kevin McCaighy who was penning at the time for *Soundsphere Magazine*:

ARAB ON RADAR – 'SUNSHINE FOR SHADY PEOPLE'
BY SOUNDSPHERE MAGAZINE – JANUARY 6, 2011

On June 2, 2002, I was still earning my stripes as a fan of underground music when I attended an Arab On Radar gig at the much-missed venue The Adelphi hotel in Leeds. Nothing could have prepared me for what I was to endure: four enraged figures dressed in sinister black prowling around the non-existent stage and surrounding amps and PA, leaping and throwing themselves into the most contorted physical shapes as they unleashed a withering torrent of sonic abuse. The band's sound was one of calculated aggravation. High frequency distortion and disassembled fragments of song, punctuated by waspish, scatological outbursts from a frenzied mouth-piece. It created an atmosphere so thick with tension that by the end of the gig mind had been comprehensively wrecked.

Arab On Radar began life in 1994 in Providence, Rhode Island, a hotbed of underground noise rock that would, in the last decade of the 20th century herald a new breed of inspired and borderline-deranged bands such as Pink & Brown, Mindflayer, Quintron, The Locust and the awesome Lightning Bolt. The story goes that the members of AOR – Eric Paul (vocals), Jeff Schneider (guitar), Steve Mattos (guitar) and Craig Kureck (drums) met when applying for jobs at a submarine manufacturing company. Despite missing out on employment, the friendship generated a new band, and with the addition of Andrea Fiset on bass, the early line-up was complete.

The documentary 'Sunshine For Shady People' attempts to place AOR in their proper context, and to give voice to a band since lost to the underground that spawned it. Rather than being an exercise in mere nostalgia, it is a ferocious prompt, a bitter reminder of the strength that lies in the undertow, that great musical diaspora, waiting for the chance to strike at a willing recipient. Nothing about the group is enshrined; in fact they were often reviled by their very own fans, friends and contemporaries. Their confrontational attitude is there for all to see as clip after devastating clip of their visceral live performance is woven into a loosely structured narrative. But the core of the documentary is a group interview shot around a kitchen table. The ex-members still remain in good terms and collaborate on projects with each other to this day. Footage of recording their second album 'Rough Day At The Orifice' in what looks like an abandoned cellar is interspersed with a litany of war stories from various tours. When faced with the choice of enjoying Oktoberfest or visiting Dachau, the band visits the concentration camp – in the pouring rain. A promoter pays them in LSD instead of cash.

A fan sculpts a clay model of Schneider's head while the band sleeps. The only note of rancor occurs when the legendary 'Oops!' tour is brought up, an adventure that included AOR alongside many of the noise-rock luminaries of the age, like Wolf Eyes, Lightning Bolt and Erase Errata: "Everyone else became stars and we broke up!" AOR's split in 2002 would make them as strangers to that kind of success, but their real legacy can be seen in the voluminous live material includes among the DVD'S extras – four (sometimes five) black-clad denizens *of an endless series of basements and run-down stages, hurling their bodies at a stream of serrated clatter and white noise, possessed as if by lightning itself. As Mattos says, they created some "righteous sh**", and left it for us to discover. Rumours of a reformation abound. Let's hope it's true?*

For more information visit the official MySpace.

Chapter 21 - Tissues, On The House

Also around this time, there was a major surge in poster art in Providence; there were so many great artists, too many to name. Sasha Wiseman, a local artist at the time, exhibited the work of many of the best artists in Providence with her Poster Art show titled "Wunderground," which achieved *New York Times* recognition. We delicately entered this RISD cathedral and saw all the usual faces, but then there were just busloads of geriatric art patrons from New York filing in. We felt as old as they looked, and we all acted the same, like granny at a tag sale, we poked and pondered, looked at tags, looked at our own music being played on a cassette player and our name on half of the posters; but it was all usurped, co-opted by greater human beings than us, more vibrant humans, richer, better creams had gone on their skin since the day they were born. If the love their parents gave them each and every day, that support, if someone like me had that for even one hour of my life I could have accomplished more than they have in their whole lives; this is the poverty and art dilemma. Pain is a gasoline, this is how the engine runs. They are just attendants but not tonight, to all these people they were great artists. I felt sick, I needed my diaper changed and some ginger ale, perhaps a few saltine crackers before I did a crossword puzzle and was hoisted into bed. I didn't care where my walker was, so stop asking.

A few years later I was living in a big loft in Providence. We had many great parties here. I would stand on the roof naked at night staring at the city and the police department one block away.

I had begun playing with a new band Made in Mexico. I was thinking about music from Peru and did not have contact with many people in the scene who would have been around when I played in Arab On Radar. I went into the musical land of Juaneco y su Combo for a while somehow, which is a very great place to be.

In 2010 we had what we called a "reunion." Regardless of our differences we met like Dons in *The Godfather*, had a sit-down meeting at this Mexican restaurant named Tortilla Flats, and instantaneously I think everyone got on board with playing again, or at least I did. We got manic in our ideas, if I had to rank them I'd say we wanted to: play shows again as Arab On Radar, learn our old songs verbatim, practice often, stay in touch, write new songs, record an album of new shit, get interest going again, maybe get a bigger group of people invested in this project. We went down to my future wife's grandparents' house, next door to a mansion, got on the new blue colored uniforms we selected (we did a different color Dickies uniform for each epoch of the band) and for this phase we had swords! Real swords, and there is a halfway decent image of us launching into battle in front of this mansion on the ocean with our swords. We agreed to hire our friend Jasmine as our road manager; she was funny, cool, and into cool music, so it seemed to be a good fit. I kept trying to tell her all of my problems, it was amazing how artful she was at subtly letting me know she did not want to be my fucking therapist. She was a really unique person, super healthy and intelligent. She reminded us all a lot of what it was like to have Andrea in the band. I think we missed those days and it was great to have

Jasmine around in her own right. Everyone was real happy it seemed. We did most of that list, but in the end we fell the fuck apart. Every show was great on that brief trip.

ARAB ON RADAR – 2010 REUNION TOUR DATES

7/2/2010 – Easthampton, MA - The Flywheel w/ Weasel Walter's Cellular Chaos and Fat Worm of Error
7/3/2010 – Providence, RI – AS220 w/ Tinsel Teeth and Whore Paint
7/10/2010 – Indianapolis, IN – ES Jungle: Dude Fest
7/23/2010 – Baltimore, MD - Whartscape
7/30/2010 – New Haven, Connecticut – Cafe Nine w/ No Babies, Orange Coax, Brava Spectre
7/31/2010 – New York, NY – The Cake Shop w/ Child Abuse, No Babies, Orange Coax
8/6/2010 – Montreal, Quebec – Lambi w/ Aids Wolf, dd/mm/yyyy
8/7/2010 – Toronto, ON – The Garrison w/ dd/mm/yyyy
8/8/2010 – Rochester, NY – The Bug Jar
9/2/2010 – San Francisco, CA – The Eagle Tavern w/ Thee Oh Sees, No Babies CANCELLED
9/3/2010 – Los Angeles, CA – The Eagle Tavern w/ 400 Blows, Foot Village and Naomi Elizabeth CANCELLED
9/4/2010 – San Diego, CA – TBD CANCELLED
9/5/2010 – Los Angeles, CA – The Smell w/ All Leather and XBXRX CANCELLED

We played at AS220 in our hometown Providence. At that loft I lived in with my wife, we hosted the after-party; hundreds of people flowed through our echo-y room. One guy was carted off in an ambulance after accidentally walking in the neighbor's door and getting punched in the face by the MMA bros who lived there. We made orange sherbet punch in bowls and projected vintage porn in 16mm on our 30' wall. People did coke all over the bathroom, scratched the shit out of our vanity and clogged the drains. It was all very exciting and we were happy to entertain anyone who wanted to be there to celebrate with Arab On Radar.

Whartscape was Dan Deacon's festival, he was cool, I always associated him with a guy named Atom and His Package, they just overlapped and I am sorry but I got confused back then. Dan had something to do with Wham City, which for all intents and purposes was the Fort Thunder of Baltimore, but 10 years later. Baltimore, what a great place, it's funny how sometimes the videotape just plays before your eyes. No fast-forward, no rewind, just playing at its own pace. I watched myself completely reject a great situation that could have happened with my wife, her very attractive art school colleague, and the singer of a great major label band from Baltimore whose name I won't reveal. It was at this "reunion" show in Baltimore. I thought I deserved more than the floor and rented a very fancy room at a French hotel near the venue ahead of time. We chilled there before the show, full bar, big bed, smelled very good, almost like a rosehips garden. All time slowed down, romance, but somehow I, in my arrogance, managed to say all the wrong things, self-destruct, didn't appreciate the mindfulness moment, wasn't present, too involved, couldn't read the poetry of the situation. And the tape played on and eventually it hit the end of the reel. Rewound at warp speed, then it was all history. I'm not sure what happened or why. When they say depression I guess this is real as it could be. Nothing left but the music and the flesh left behind. Never became anything, and it was all my fault. I suppose there is a French word for "the blues" but I don't know it...

We came out of the Rochester, NY show dejected; an embarrassing tiff broke out on stage between Craig and Steve, things fell apart. In the end I think I was a baboon from another troop, this time around we did not marry, only dated, then the Patrol Squad of 3 male adolescents came out to pummel me. The reason Arab On Radar broke up is purely Nature and Biology. I had moved on up in the hierarchy of primates and they had gone in another direction, none of us could be anything other than what we had become in life and we were no longer compatible people.

Years had past, we still delivered the goods... although post-rehab those two guys lacked the chutzpah we once had, tattooing your own poetry on yourself, how crazy... There were times I reminisce about these people I played in Arab On Radar with, on a good day some were *poets*, brothers, on a bad day, psychopaths that I had fallen prey to; I had catered to their narcissistic traits for years. I am not sure where the truth lies about these matters. I know we could never do it again, never play in Arab On Radar again, and I am sorry for that. I feel bad we couldn't get the last unrecorded album out, it was wicked good and who knows what may have come next? Be careful being too smart or too dumb, you need to be just right, moderation, because a few IQ points make all the difference.

The break-up at the end after the reunion was not pretty, the pot heated up before the water boiled as there were a few micro-aggressions going on, you know, things like, as a total joke my posting on Facebook saying that we were going to be playing the *Jimmy Fallon Show* in New York, and of course, you know, very few people liked the post, they thought it was funny, a joke. But Craig got really upset with me, offended, days later at practice he was almost crying. He confronted me with stories from his friends from Emerson he went to film school with, the richest people in the world were his roommates, you know, the niece of Philippines dictator Ferdinand Marcos and Bernadette Peters' nephew, people who had lived in Manhattan their whole lives, never ever left Manhattan. These people were emailing him saying, "Congratulations, I know Jimmy, I'm so glad you can meet him, you'll see, he's a really cool guy" and yadda yadda, his family was saying, "You finally made it." Which really highlighted the absurdity of how we had worked for all these years, a span of twenty years, and still there was such a huge stretch for us ever to be able to play a mainstream show like that, we could've shown up at the door, gear in hand demanding to play, pirate tactics, something which we had been joking about at practice, the post was an allusion to this. Craig's devastation made me just shake my head like, what? I felt like I brushed up against his wall of denial, and in truth I felt really bad for the guy. We had planned to record a demo of new songs to bring on the West Coast tour and had studio time lined up with Weasel Walter.

Those guys decided last minute to cancel the recording session and Craig argued with me *relentlessly* but without ever giving a reason why other than that he didn't want to do it. Twenty texts back and forth, talk about a "toxic relationship with me," I woke up to an "I'm done with you" text from Eric, I realized that the West Coast tour dates had also been cancelled without me knowing it. The band never met in person for a reality check amidst this ego-driven insane text war. It all was very petty, stuff that could've been smoothed over rather than spiraling out of control. Alas, no divorce attorney was paid to settle custody over the music, the band, these new commitments, tour promises unfulfilled. Perhaps having a scapegoat to blame the destruction of Arab On Radar on was more valuable to them, more conducive to carrying on our legacy under a new band name.

The interim between the break up and the reunion was a toxic relationship with Eric and Craig. They were in the Chinese Stars and became completely the worst alcoholic drug addict stereotypes, I won't disclose the extent of their clinical treatment, but it was intense. They went on party tours declaring a jihad on the legacy of Arab On Radar and me personally, talking shit about me obsessively and burning every bridge we ever built. Old friends were listening to this bullshit, some fools even believed it. They were under the spell of addiction. You can read interviews they did on the West Coast after the second break up, their new coke friends in San Diego writing articles trashing me, it was pretty obvious, it was very hurtful to read the social media posts of so-called friends just buying the lies. They Judas'd me, and assuming no blame whatsoever, went around spreading their narrative to a wide group of believers.

The reunion was walking on eggshells, I swear, but are you surprised? I completely forgave and forgot and just went back into that reunion with all I had, but what was apparent towards the end of that short reunion was we were just in two different places in life. I had a career after grad school, so much had happened. They were under this frenzied spell that they would make it in music someday and it would pay all their bills and provide lifetime health insurance and a pension. I long ago said to myself that this is not the way it works in Life, no free rides. People can judge for themselves, if they see any musicians the likes of Arab On Radar out there living in mansions, just let me know who they are, I probably know them, I'll have to go by for tea sometime. If you are going to be an innovator, particularly in Music, you will live in squalor and your heart will be carved out like a pumpkin on the night before Halloween.

I think of Jesus Christ, probably some righteous guy at the time, he healed, fought off all loss to the little guy. But, look at what people worship. Political heats up and then there is a backlash, a pendulum of pressure. People start standing on street corners, in major cities, shouting about their newspaper, or on the other side, fucking Hari Krishna. We tapped into that, whatever it is, "cult emotions," Superego blessings, Id energy, Ego making a reason to believe. Perhaps they liked the violence. Ultimately, those guys died a creative death worse than death itself, one of being sentenced to beta status, mediocrity, contemporary Antonio Salieris... I suppose it had to be. The music scene itself dissipated, everyone graduated high school, the times changed. I've always argued that the generation gap and its drastic differences was as great between the 1950s "Greatest Generation" and the Boomers/Hippies as it was from us Gen-Xers to Millenials. The period of 1965 – 2009 was just a neutral, fertile zone, and the Rock Music Community prospered in its mossy, wet environment. The Identity Politics movement when applied to our scene was, musically speaking, nothing more than the fragmentation of the Musical Identity; now the prefixes are all that are left in tact. Some of these fragments are not all that positive. I don't think it will end well, musically or socially. Many go on, they are doing something in this mess, playing in a cover band, it is nothing more than a tribute to a greater time.

The plane came in for a landing. I may have been hallucinating from the extreme heat, but I vividly recall a young child walking over to the garage where I sat writing in the middle of summer. This child looked very Scandinavian, perhaps a hippy's kid, wearing a long dress or robe, they carried flowers, yellow daisies in a bunch in their hand, they approached and asked "What are you doing?" in the most innocent tone. I replied, "If I could only begin to explain…" They puzzled me and I knew my answer would only puzzle them. It sometimes takes a book to make a point. It is important to keep asking people this question, "What are you doing?" What are you doing Musically, Creatively, Artistically and otherwise, because you never know whom exactly you are talking to, or what their deal may be. The answer may be something; their deal may be something great and as unknown as this story.

People ask me, "What the fuck do you do nowadays?" I am embracing the things I enjoy. I am lucky because somehow I transitioned from having a job, compelled labor for money, to a career, something I would do voluntarily. I have children and my wife. Perhaps this seems to be the witness protection program but I do not think so. I am old now and things do change, if they don't then you are fucked in my opinion. Live your life and stay in tune with the direction in which you develop; be honest.

Navigating the basics was not always easy. If you forgot your backpack of clothes, which included your towel, many survivalist choices had to be made. Should I use the one on the towel rack at the squat? Was there one? I have rolled up a person's floor mat that surrounded their toilet to dry off once. Toothbrushes, forget it, if that item was out in the van, in a bag, five miles away wherever we parked, the ones that were seen were used. I have used many people's toothbrushes without their knowledge and I would like to formally apologize for that. I have wiped my nether-region on people's sheets, on their pillowcases, on their shirts from their bureau. Shame on me for that. Many times you just stayed wet, because drying off with your moldy towel would only defeat the purpose. I have many times used armpit deodorant of many sexes, smelling of Secret, it was my favorite scent at one point on tour. We'd eat people's food because we were broke, totally untrustworthy. It wasn't an easy life being a vulture on tour, flying amongst the eagles and the pigeons, but we survived. These basic toiletries are very important, especially when you're at the therapist's office crying and she hands you the box of tissues.

THE END

BIRTH...
COCAINE
GOD IS DEAD
ASTHMA
NATHAN
FATHER
MUFFLER

Epilogue

In the process of writing the book about Arab On Radar I decided to interview many people, some of the "key players" in the band's history. I am deeply saddened to find out that an old friend, a person on the list to talk to passed away. Jason Swanson was this guy's name. He met us a long time ago as a booking agent on some of AOR's first tour stops, most connections in the Grand Rapids, MI area were all formed through Jason. The really sad part is that we considered him part of the family. I can't explain what an amazing person he was or how much I looked forward to "just making it to Jason and Sue's house" after many hours on the road, they provided respite for us in their home and we sincerely loved them. Sue was Jason's girlfriend at the time, she was, and I do not mean this in any sexist way, a beautiful looking person, she looked like the supermodel Rachel Hunter back in the day. Sue was a very mothering person, really intelligent and peaceful. She was always cool with us (in our ragged state) and very much one of the guys. Another fascinating thing is their love for one another. I am not exaggerating, these two expressed such a deep love, so together, for us weirdos this was a thing we respected and of course we never tried any funny business with Sue. They seemed to love each other on a level I never knew could be, a rarity, but it was so obvious. I remember that they also cared for rescue dogs. I think they had two pit bulls, one he kept in the bedroom, because it was a bit feisty, and I was terrified when it came out (irrationally) but I recall thinking, "man he is a Native American, they communicate with Nature and shit, he knows somehow this dog won't bite me," typical ignorant mindset that I had at the time, but nonetheless, funny and something we laughed at, real hard. He/they loved these dogs and rehabilitated them from a presumably traumatized state. Jason, man, all I can say is that he spoke and had the aura of Bob Marley, perhaps it is his facial feature; but then again, he spoke softly like Bob did and had a shamanic presence about him. I remember commenting on this to him and he discussed his Native American heritage. He was joking saying, "Man, my mom is all into this shit, so I do it." But another time he told me about the "nipple ritual" which I am sure is something very sacred and I mean no disrespect, but it was something we laughed very hard about almost peeing our pants, ya know, Jason hanging suspended from his man-tits was a joke back then. We smoked a lot of grass, he always had the "purple shit" which was just splendid, it eased our stressed minds, we felt like we were home, or better than home, a place where we always belonged. I vividly recall lamenting that "man, if I could have just one big party, one big cookout and invite all the coolest people we met from all over the world..." Jason was high up on that list when I had those thoughts. Alas, and to the shame of my former band-mates who at best did not know this, at worst, are so childish they just never told me, I found out this morning that my old friend has passed away, some sort of heart-attack, back in 2012. It is totally my fault for being Rip Van Winkle on this, I admit to checking out since then and avoiding social media. Even at the end of AOR Jason and Sue, I think, kind of outgrew us, they went on with life and we went on to later tours, bigger shows etc. but these guys were there since the beginning and I was thoroughly looking forward to talking with Jason about what the hell we all were doing back in the 90's when we were close. I suppose that conversation will have to wait. Good-bye old buddy, and I hope Sue and all of your family are well. I am sorry for not finding this out sooner, but then again, what matters most is the fun times we had together and the gift you gave me by having met you and the wonderful person you are. Thanks for that.

ABOUT THE AUTHOR

Jeff Schneider, aka Mr. Clinical Depression, is a writer, musician, and artist. He gained recognition in the 1990s for playing guitar in the noise rock band Arab On Radar. The band was signed to Skin Graft Records and ThreeOneG Records respectively. Jeff went on to form the band Made in Mexico that gained critical acclaim for being in the original video games Guitar Hero and Guitar Hero II. Touring for over 15 years world-wide, writing and recording 6 full-length albums, multiple 7'' recordings, compilations, and splits with some of the finest underground noise musicians and record labels of his time, Jeff has shifted focus to writing. Founding Pig Roast Publishing, LLC was a new endeavor aimed at collaborating with the weirdest, most interesting writers, and helping them produce quality books that reach the *special* readers who appreciate the spirit of No-Wave, Noise, Punk Rock, and keeping the DiY ethic alive.

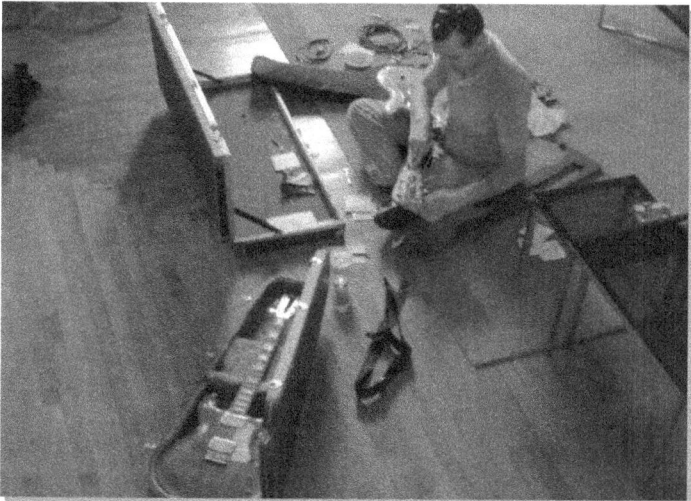